Very lovingly yours,

Elsie

Barbara
Anne
Waite

Memoirs compiled by
Barbara Anne Waite

Adventures of an
Arizona Schoolteacher
1913–1916

Elsie: Adventures of an Arizona Schoolteacher 1913-1916
Library of Congress Control Number: 2011918600
ISBN: 978-0-9839452-0-8

Cover and text design by Diane King, www.dkingdesigner.com

Published by Palomar Mountain Bookworks
　　　　　2382 Primrose Ave. Vista, Ca. 92083

barbaraannewaite.com

Printed in the United States of America.

Contents

Introduction

Tears. Tears softly falling over her sweet wrinkled face. Tears that I had caused. I had never seen her cry. I had never even heard her complain or be angry. My grandmother had always been a source of joy in my life. Now I had brought tears to her eyes.

It had been such a simple question. For years I had heard her joyful stories of teaching in Arizona when she was in her twenties. Often she fondly recalled the adventure of living in a wild new state. But now there were tears in that memory. Tears. . . because I had asked, "Did you ever love anyone before my grandfather?" I had innocently probed and uncovered a deeply buried hurt that I had never dreamed was there. So I hugged her and said, "Please don't cry, Grammy."

"There was this cowboy. . . " She said simply and then stopped.

I could not bear to ask why a memory from so long ago still brought tears. Elsie's Arizona story was one of great joy in the adventures her life had held. But now I understood there was also a deeply buried sorrow that she had never shared. The mystery of that sorrow was only intensified when I read her writings after her death.

"I loved and still love Arizona. . ." The detailed, well-crafted, handwritten manuscript did not appear to be the work of someone who was almost ninety-seven years old. It was my grandmother, Elsie Reed Hayes Roberts' final manuscript—a project she never completed. A year after her death I discovered the manuscript nestled among her many published short stories and articles. Never before had she written anything that stirred me like this unfinished story of love and adventure in the fledgling State of Arizona.

Most people have heard the expression, "Even if I live to a hundred, I'll never forget. . ." My Grandmother Elsie lived to be nearly one hundred years old. The years spent in Arizona had clearly been unforgettable. She left a record of those memorable years—from 1913 to1916—in her diary and in about thirty letters written home from the new state of Arizona. The diary and letters reveal the dramatic story of a vivacious, charming young teacher who was loved by her students as well as by a couple of Arizona's adventurous young men.

As a child I always thought of Elsie as prim and proper . . . and *old*. I loved her dearly; everyone who knew Elsie loved her. She was a master storyteller, and my earliest recollections of her are the stories she told in a soft, whispery, yet dramatic voice. Most grandchildren go to grandmother's house for home-cooked meals. I don't remember Elsie's cooking, but I do remember her stories. When I cleaned her house for her, she would usually be curled up on the couch, writing. Soon, instead of my working, I would be listening to one of her fascinating stories—a tale of her childhood, a Civil War event she had heard from her father. Elsie wrote and published many magazine stories, poems, and articles over the years. As a child I delighted in reading these outpourings of my grandmother's life and imagination. She spent her life helping others to love literature.

It was after her death in 1987 that I first picked up her well-worn black leather diary, not realizing it would reveal a young Elsie whom I had never imagined. The diary told of her first love, of heartache and sorrow, and of fascinating adventure. Never had I pictured my grandmother as being free-spirited, young, and in love. My curiosity was stirred, and I began to search for more records of her Arizona years.

Her diary could not give me all the answers, but hidden in a library archive was the answer to those tears. Piece by piece, through letters, newspaper articles, and the diary, her story deepened.

Elsie frequently described her Arizona years as "glorious." She experienced isolation, lack of modern conveniences, and sacrifice—nevertheless, still she remembered and described those days as delightful. But the tears were also a part of that remembrance. As I read her diaries and her letters written home to California I saw why she had great joy in the memory of those years. Only later did the discovery of an old newspaper article give me the answer I had been longing to find. But this is not a sorrowful story—it is, like Elsie, delightful—a mirror into her exuberance and zest for life in early Arizona. As you will discover, she had a heart that refused to focus on the hard things; instead, she focused on the joy found in the adventure of a challenge.

Eventually my search for more information led me to write the newspaper office in Cottonwood, Arizona in 1988. Neighboring Cornville, where

Elsie first taught, had remained too small for a newspaper. Writing to any newspaper to ask for information about Elsie seemed futile. After all, she had lived there less than a year, and that had been seventy-five years before.

I soon discovered that, just as Cornville's Oak Creek had been unforgettable for Elsie, she, too, had been unforgettable for her students. The very first of a number of responses to my newspaper letter amazed me. I began to cry as I read a letter from "darling, adorable, dainty, little Eva," with whom my grandmother had lived on Shadyvale Ranch in 1913. "Little Eva," as my grandmother had called her, was now eighty-four years old and still living on the ranch. Eva Girdner Stone wrote,

> I certainly do remember Elsie Hayes. She was my third grade teacher and I loved her! She roomed and boarded with my folks and taught in a two-roomed school on our ranch. The area here was very primitive at that time and my folks wondered how the teachers could ever adjust to our ways of living. But your grandmother, especially, adjusted beautifully. I remember just how she looked, the color of her hair, etc. I could tell you lots of stories that I still remember of things that happened while "Miss Hayes" lived here. They would be as seen through eyes of an eight year old of course! Your letter in our local paper caused quite a stir amongst the old timers here! It seems impossible that all this could happen. A memory only, has become alive after 75 years!

I felt I must meet Little Eva and see Elsie's Oak Creek for myself. The clear view on the day in 1988 that I flew to Arizona to meet Eva was spectacular. I imagined how very different my aerial view of Oak Creek was from Elsie's view from the stagecoach, so many years earlier. Oak Creek Canyon was beautiful and such a romantic spot. I could picture Elsie sitting on the roots of her favorite sycamore tree beside the creek reading poetry; I could visualize her bathing in the creek in her "old, pink, crepe dress." I began to understand why the Arizona years were so unforgettable for her.

I, too, soon loved Elsie's Little Eva. She was as charming in person as in her letter. I met several other former students who vividly remembered Elsie and had stories to tell that harmonized with her diary and letters home. My picture of life in the brand-new State of Arizona was becoming clearer and more exciting.

The Sharlot Hall Library in Prescott allowed me to read issues of their *Yavapai Monthly Magazine* dated 1913 to 1916. The library in the capitol building in Phoenix gave me access to the Jerome newspaper for the same time period. Eva Girdner Stone shared some of the articles her brother Dale had written for *Westward* magazine. They told of his memories of early Arizona and even recalled his teacher Elsie Hayes. Later, in Williams, the librarian opened the small library there for me. Soon I felt lost in Elsie's Arizona years, and I longed to know more about this adventurous young woman who found love on America's frontier.

I came across a tape recording Elsie had made for the Jerome Historical Society. On the tape she said in closing, "I don't see how people who have lived in Arizona's Verde Valley or the mountains, even briefly, can bear to live in a real city." Elsie, in fact, lived in a "real city" for most of her seventy-one years after she left Arizona. Perhaps she lived on memories of her time in Oak Creek Canyon and Williams, memories kept fresh by rereading her daily journals and letters to her family.

I have left her letters and diary in this book as she wrote them, only editing out unrelated events. I used additional narrative in brackets taken from my conversations with her, cassette tapes, manuscripts, recollections from her former students, and her own oral stories. It is those conversations, stories, and recollections that have also provided material for the chapter introductions.

Arizona from 1913 to 1916 was a wild and wonderful place. Here are memories of that infant state as seen through the eyes of this delightful, spirited, young teacher.

Who's Who

Elsie's family

- Elsie Hayes (sometimes signed her letters "Sylvia")
- Alonzo Hayes, Elsie's father

- May Carrie Hayes, Elsie's mother
- Aunt Mamie, Alonzo's sister
- Alice, Elsie's younger sister (sometimes referred to as "Paddy")
- Hylinda, Elsie's older sister
- Ernest Burley, Alice's fiancé
- Dorothy Burley, Alice and Ernest Burley's baby
- Fritz, Elsie's dog

Elsie's friends in California

- Ruth Stailey, Caroline Harnett (along with Elsie, known as "the Triumvirate")
- Helen Hogle
- Kenneth Darling
- Dr. & Mrs. A.V. Stoughton (Pomona College physician 1911–1924)
- Alice M. Parker (A. M. P.), Elsie's Pomona college professor, mentor, and confidante
- Fanny Hand

In Cornville

- Mr. and Mrs. Girdner and children Dale, Glen, Stanley, and Eva (Elsie lived on their ranch.)
- Karl Hurst, his mother, and step-father
- Mr. Ferguson ("Fergy")

Elsie's colleagues

- Marguerite Melick, Elsie's fellow teacher and roommate in Cornville
- Eugene Barron (Red Rocks teacher)

Elsie's students in Cornville

- Walter Fenstermaker, Bessie Lee, Edgar Lee, Myrtle Stewart, Elon Stewart, David Wiley Stewart, Fern Stewart, Frank Flores, Rosie Flores, Della Flores, Columbus (Lum) Farley, Riola Phillips, Elwin Van Deren, Myrtle Van Deren, Lovina Topping, Ruth Hurst, Jessie Duncan, Doris Johnson, Nellie Smith, Della Smith, Eva Girdner, Stanley Girdner, Dale Girdner, Glen Girdner, Mildred Finney, Sarah Stuck, Locus Hayden, Reymundo

In Williams 1914-16

- Minna Wissing, Elsie's roommate
- Mr. Frank McCrae Gold, lawyer
- W. W. Bass, Grand Canyon guide
- John John Planwydd ("Jack") Roberts
- Mr. Craig (in Phoenix)

Elsie's Southern California and Arizona locations

1

Quite the Adventure!

"I donned old clothes and hurried to the creek for a bath before dinner. The water felt perfectly scrumptious. I wore my pink crepe for a bathing suit. . . and lay on my back on the rocks."

The motion of the train must have strengthened for Elsie Hayes the realization that she was moving away from home and things familiar and heading for a year of change and adventure. Although born in Alexandria, Virginia, she still considered herself to be a Westerner because she had lived in California for the last fourteen of her twenty-five years. Never having been to Arizona, she looked forward with great expectation to her arrival in this unfamiliar, wild land. Elsie was also thankful that she was not alone. The California teachers' agency had arranged for her to travel from Los Angeles to the farming town of Cornville, Arizona, with her fellow teacher Marguerite Melick.

The last twenty-six miles of their journey by train was from the Santa Fe main line near Prescott via the narrow-gauge United Verde and Pacific Railroad. It was a trying combination of twists and turns as the train crept up the steep mountain grade, and the girls had heard jokes about the train being so slow that anyone could get off to pick wildflowers and get back on again. It was not a trip for the faint of heart or stomach; they could expect 186 sharp curves. The line ended at Jerome, on the east slope of Mingus Mountain. Wealthy financier Eugene Jerome, for whom the town was named, had built the narrow-gauge United Verde and Pacific Railroad in 1893 to haul ore from the copper mines, and at one time Jerome had been the third-largest town in Arizona. Elsie and Marguerite heard people on the train talking about the mining town, and someone remarked that Jerome was "the wickedest town in America." From there, a stagecoach would take them the following day to Cornville in the lush Verde Valley below.

In California Elsie had grown up in the emerging city of Long Beach, but she had enjoyed the rural wildness of summers on Palomar Mountain in San Diego County, where her father had an apple ranch. She was accustomed to the rugged three-and-a-half-day trip by horse and wagon from Long Beach to Palomar. Though rugged, those wagon trips were full of adventure and charm for Elsie, so the adventure of sleeping out of doors under the stars and creating a bed from straw meant for the horses was not a trial. She even believed that those adventures on Palomar Mountain had prepared her for her upcoming life in rural Arizona. She hoped to find a horse to ride after settling, for she had already been told not to expect any automobiles in Cornville. It was just too rough and undeveloped for such luxuries. After all, Arizona had become a state only the year before, in 1912. But, thankfully, Elsie was not merely accustomed to riding a horse—she delighted in it.

As this attractive, self-assured young teacher talked with the young woman beside her, Elsie wondered whether Miss Melick would adjust easily to the rough, wild adventure of Arizona life. Though Marguerite said she had lived for some time on her sister's Wisconsin farm, it was equipped with "modern" conveniences. The teachers' agency had tried to prepare them for life with no electricity or running water. This lack of conveniences could prove to be a difficult obstacle to overcome for someone such as Marguerite, who was not used to roughing it. However, if not emotionally prepared, Marguerite physically looked sturdy enough for country life, perhaps even more so than Elsie, who appeared to be somewhat fragile.

Dedicated and serious, Elsie had worked hard in high school and was the valedictorian of Long Beach High in 1907. But she had also listened to the doctor when he had told her not to work so hard in college. She had even stayed out of college for two years to rest up and become strong enough to

Left—Elsie Hayes, Valedictorian, Long Beach High 1907; Top right—Long Beach High 1907; Bottom right—Elsie's Long Beach home

finish the vigorous academic schedule. Having just graduated from Pomona College in Claremont, California, she couldn't help her feelings of regret that her years there had come to an end. She had loved the professors and the social activities, but Pomona was not a teachers' college, and she was planning on a fifth year at the University of California at Berkeley to obtain her teacher's training. However, lacking funds for the year at Berkeley, she had decided that the opportunity to teach in Arizona would benefit her financially and physically. So here she was on her way not to Berkeley but to undeveloped Arizona and a one-room school.

In spite of her college degree, Elsie had some doubts about her own abilities as a teacher, since she had no experience and knew little about methods. Still, her temporary worry did not crowd out her joy at finally being able to teach. Her high school annual had predicted of Elsie Hayes, paraphrasing Chaucer, "And gladly wolde (she) lerne, and gladly teche." Elsie loved literature and yearned to help others appreciate it as well, so she naturally felt some disappointment that Marguerite had been assigned the older students and she had the five younger grades. However, since Marguerite was older and had more experience, Elsie simply looked forward to the years ahead when her teaching experience would allow her to teach high school English grammar and literature, her real loves.

It was Saturday and late afternoon as the two expectant teachers approached the city, which was perched on the side of a beautiful mountain. However, the beauty of the mountain held little interest for the girls—they had heard too much about the area's dangerous underground excavations and were feeling very nervous about this part of their journey. It had been reported that eighty-seven miles of tunnels ran beneath the town. The train station, located next to the mine, was some distance from the town because of these excavations. Thus, a mule-drawn stagecoach was to meet the girls and give them a harrowing ride down the steep, narrow, winding mountain road to the town.

Elsie spent a frightening night in Jerome—the streets were filled with "foreigners, drunken men, and Indians wrapped in blankets." She and Marguerite were eager to leave the next morning for Cornville. The narrow road down Mingus Mountain, descending two thousand feet to the Verde Valley, was a nerve-racking experience, and the girls were much relieved to reach the valley where they were to live.

The small town of Cottonwood, which they passed on their way down to the valley, had looked a little barren; however, as they approached the area where Oak Creek joined the Verde River they were awed by the beauty of the lush valley. Still, they had not yet grasped how undeveloped Cornville would be. There was nothing there but a very small post office that also served as the only store for many miles around. Spreading out along the creek were the valley's farms.

Nonetheless, the girls were impressed by the first family they met in Cornville. The Girdner children were eager to meet the new teachers. It was here in the family's yard that the teachers were to live in a small shack prepared especially for the girls. It was not much of a home, but it would give them some privacy and a place of their own.

The Girdner family had explained that they had come to the Arizona territory in 1907. They recalled for Elsie how the year before, when statehood was granted to Arizona, there were about twenty-five families living along the lower Oak Creek. Statehood was celebrated by the families all gathering for a picnic. Mrs. Girdner made a special dress for her young daughter Eva using red, white and blue material. The children celebrated with foot and burro races.

In previous years they had had only had one teacher for all eight grades. However, the grades would now be divided between the two teachers. The family seemed to be pleased that the state, as well as their little rural school, was now progressing.

After the family left the girls on their own to settle in, Elsie saw the despair on Marguerite's face. She had begun to question Elsie about drinking water, how they would take a bath with no tub, and how they would wash clothes. Elsie knew Marguerite wanted to teach these farm children and hoped she would adjust, but she recognized that the surroundings might easily overwhelm her. She had explained to Elsie that the only laundry she had ever done was to wash out a handkerchief. Elsie had always focused on the beauty found in nature and cared little about where she slept or ate or about the difficulties of bathing and washing laundry.

Neither did the appearance of the one-room schoolhouse serve to reassure Marguerite. It was a plain, unpainted wooden structure with a large wood stove; there was little about it that was attractive. It had a movable partition that divided the one room into two, and the lighting for both the shack and the school came from coal-oil lamps. The girls were told that the ugly brown stains running down the walls were where cowboys had spit tobacco juice when the school was used for local dances.

This year of 1913 was not going to be easy. Elsie learned of the strict rules for Arizona's teachers:

- Teachers are not to keep company with men.
- Women may not dye their hair.
- Two petticoats must be worn.
- Teachers may not loiter downtown in ice cream stores.
- Dresses must be no more than two inches above the ankle.
- Teachers are not to dress in bright colors.

Though teaching here would be a very real challenge, Elsie had been captivated by the rugged beauty of the canyon and the creek; she knew there would be adjustments, but nonetheless she was filled with excitement and anticipation.

Elsie's family; Ernest Burley, Alice, Hylinda, Alonzo Hayes, Elsie, Aunt Mamie, May Carrie Hayes, and Dorothy Burley

In spite of this, Elsie knew she would miss her close-knit family. She had been away from them while at college and knew she would experience home-sickness now, as she had then. Her younger sister, Alice, was so busy with her fiancé, Ernest, that she had not seen much of her that past summer. English-born Ernest Burley would be good for Alice (he had a wonderful voice and traveled for years as a soloist with an evangelist), and Elsie loved him already, but it would be hard to lose her closest sister. Hylinda was Elsie's older sister and had never been as close to her as had Alice. Elsie would also miss her dear Aunt Mamie as much as she would her papa or her mother. Aunt Mamie, Papa's sister, never married and had been a part of Elsie's family for almost as long as she could remember. Aunt Mamie loved telling stories, and her quaint sayings were so much fun that they had endeared her to everyone. Elsie had promised her beloved family that she would write often from Arizona, for let-ters would be her only link with her family for the next eight months.

Cornville, Arizona
Tuesday—6 p.m., September 9, 1913
On a log by Oak Creek

My very dear Family:

By the time this reaches Long Beach, you may all be at home. I won't write decently because the ink is bad, and also because dinner is at 6:30, and I want to tell you a lot before then! But you should see my blackboard penmanship! This is the first letter I've tried to write in Cornville.

I must tell you about Jerome. It was Saturday and late afternoon as we approached Jerome. The train stopped some distance from the town because of the dangerous underground excavations. We were told that it wasn't safe for us to go further because of the weight upon the ground. The station is beside the mine and smelter (copper is the ore). A sort of stage met the halted train and took us passengers into the town, we each paid fifty cents. I certainly wouldn't walk. The short drive is on a narrow, steep, winding mountain road.

I never imagined such a town. It looks like New York slums turned loose on a hillside and like Spain and Italy and almost like Chinatown combined. The mountainside is bare and bleak and the houses are queer and black and mysterious looking. One goes into a house (not knowing which is front, side or back) from a dirty sidewalk and muddy street, with which the balcony before the house is on a level. He follows the narrow, railed balcony around to the other side and finds he is on the second story and looking down upon other queer houses. The dirty saloons are surrounded by groups of foreigners who stare.

When we turned into the town little children of all kinds followed us waving and dancing. Such hordes of children and babies I never saw before. I saw three small boys holding babies, one holding a very wee one. Almost all are Mexican or Italian. I gave some of the left over cake in oiled paper to two dark skinned stringy-haired youngsters who were more than pleased. I want to have a big bag of candy next time, each piece in paper, you know the kind, and throw out handfuls of it!

A leaflet on the train had advertized a certain hotel, so we said we'd go there for overnight. We'd been told that the next day a stage would be going down to Cornville. Jerome is a frontier mining town and Saturday night of course meant celebration. It looked wild. The bus driver stopped at a corner where there was a saloon, with a drunken man leaning against a post in front of it. A dark narrow staircase outside led up to evident rooms above. The driver pointed. "That's the hotel up there," he said. I felt terrified and Marguerite was trembling so hard her jaw was shaking. The driver no doubt noticed our feeling for he said, "You don't have to stay there. I know a woman who takes in girls, I'll drive you there." That certainly didn't make us feel much better. I thought "white slavery" with horror.

Apparently Marguerite thought the same. She was very pale and could hardly speak as she said "We'll look at the place." I managed, "We'll look at the woman." When we discovered that a local school teacher lived there we really were relieved. The landlady was honest and kind and friendly. Saturday night meals didn't appeal to us so we got what we wanted at a clean drug store. I got a chocolate malted milk as good as those at the Wisteria.

The next day we were driven down from the mountainside by the narrow country road to the beautiful Verde valley to where (near Cornville) lower Oak Creek joins the Verde River. Oak Creek is about three minutes from the Girdners' where we live. We crossed the creek three times on the two-mile drive from the post office at Cornville. We crossed the Verde (into which this empties), I believe, on the fifteen mile stage trip from Jerome to the Cornville office. Then the rough water was above the horses knees. The stage driver said that our creek, Oak Creek, is the prettiest one in Arizona, and I don't doubt it.

Where we are sitting, it is rather deep and about as wide as from our house to Papa's office, I should think, or nearly so. Cottonwoods (large ones) and sycamores and willows border it thickly, and here and there a mass of wild grapevine covers a tree. There are low hills all around running up from the creek. From the house there is a view of the Black Hills that is wonderful. They are the only mountains I've seen in Arizona that look like the California ones. They are a rich blue and high and look nearer than the mountains do from Long Beach, but further than they look from Claremont. The clumps of trees and lines of them bordering the water make lovely views in all directions.

On the train we passed so many barren places and schoolhouses (the worst, I think, were near Cajon Pass before we were out of California), that I was prepared for a bleak outlook, and unspeakably thankful for all this beauty about us. There are Indian caves and hieroglyphics all about here that the Girdners will show us, distances of a quarter of a mile to perhaps a mile, I imagine. Also, Montezuma's Well and Montezuma's Castle are only ten, eight, twelve miles or so away. I'm eager to see all these things. We are many miles from the Petrified Forest or the Grand Canyon, however. I don't know what to tell you about first!

We kept school only half a day yesterday, but stayed ourselves until about six, and I worked much in the evening. I have a sense of leisure tonight. It was the arranging of the work and study of school laws and prescribed courses of study that swamped us at first. Today school lasted the regular length of time, nine o'clock to four o'clock, with two twenty minute recesses and an hour at noon. It takes about two minutes to walk up the hill from our house to the schoolhouse. We have to stay at noon to be with the children, but Mrs. Girdner sends us delicious luncheons, daintily prepared.

It is now about five o'clock p.m. on Wednesday. Please excuse pencil. Last night we all sat around the table and talked so long that I had no time left in the evening for anything but business. I'm so hot now that I'm sticky all over. I'm writing this time in the room we have for the present, with rafters (the new ones) overhead and not very much window space. I was prepared for things so much worse than we found them that I can take such conditions as a lark, but poor Marguerite finds country life almost too much at first! She's always lived in town, for example, and apparently never washed a thing in her life. This she has done some tonight, and she dreads taking off her silk stockings but supposes she'll have to eventually wear some other sort to school in order to be sensible! Marguerite has never taken a bath from a basin and doesn't know how she can! I think she'll get used to country life. I find things wonderfully near my ideal for this year. I shouldn't want to live here always, out of the world.

As Marguerite has the ninth grade, I have the first five instead of just four grades, as these people evidently expected all the time. I have only nine children so far in all the five grades. Ever so many more are coming next week, we hear, and others still later when they aren't needed for home work. Cattlemen who have their families with them in the mountains come here for the winter for school and to avoid the deep snow, etc. Evidently we'll have a more or less shifting registration.

Some of my children are dear and must be of good families. Others are "common" and need baths! But I think I'll love them all. Here comes a good, cool breeze. The air in here is grand, the most bracing I've ever known. It is wonderfully dry air in Arizona, you know. I think it is going to agree with me splendidly I've been feeling strikingly better than I had dared to expect for the first strenuous days after our trip. I don't at all know that you would want to come here. I'll tell you first more about our own arrangements. I like Marguerite and shall enjoy living with her.

Our first mail and my trunk here interrupted me. I was charmed to have so much, two cards from Mama and a letter with enclosures from Aunt Mamie.

The stage driver could only bring one trunk at a time from Jerome, as he has only a little two seated wagon. He brought Marguerite's because I had an extra suitcase. Mine waited for today's stage.

The Girdners are lovely Mr. Girdner is Clerk of the Board, and his wife has a keen and intelligent interest in all school matters. I think she's

Top left—Elsie's shack and the Girdner home; Top right—The Girdner family 1913; Bottom—Eva Girdner, age 8

an unusually wise mother, and the children are dear. Glen, sixteen, looks and acts like George Seely! He and Dale, who is homely but nice, both have red hair. Stanley is the youngest boy, age twelve I think, and handsome and winning, a darling. Marguerite has all of them, and I have bright dainty little Eva, the one girl aged eight. They are all lovely to us.

Mrs. Girdner is a fine cook and has sensible things to eat. I heard her say we are to have chicken and peach cobbler tonight! They have plenty of vegetables, but so far have had nothing in the way of meat but chicken and bacon. Beef seems scarce here, though there are plenty of cattle, delicious peaches and melons, and plenty of vegetables. I had milk and had a raw egg this morning for breakfast. I also had grape nuts and cream and a potato cake and stewed blackberries, and refused bacon and cooked eggs and coffee. I eat ever so much and have a fine appetite. We have to get used to going without butter, though, and we don't have napkins except in our red tin tobacco boxes in which our lunch arrives! Friday and Saturday we expect to move into a twelve by thirteen room separate from the house. They will calcimine the ceiling (which is cloth under the shingles) and repaper the walls. We are to get our own breakfasts and luncheons, but Mrs. Girdner will let us have dinners. She'd rather not get all our meals, and we can easily see to the two simple ones, I think. I'd be grateful for anything you'd think of and could get to help out!

Please send paper napkins and crush bag of mine to take to school, if you can find it. I think it's in my window seat. Please send the one I carried with my gray suit with fringe on the bottom. I'd like a tube of paste too and school crayons. Can you send us a McStay Grocery Catalog or their address? If you haven't the catalog, I'd be glad if you would write to the company to send it to us so we'd have it sooner. I've written to Sears Roebuck. Marguerite has written for her chafing dish. Please send too, the better looking of our old riding skirts. We'll have a chance to ride they say

Latest Edition! Schoolhouse, Noon, Thursday

I've thought of some more things to tell you or ask you to send. Please get me some plain side combs large enough to be used other ways. Combs bought for back combs are too large. The jolting of the Jerome stage lost mine.

Top—Elsie loved riding and described her divided skirt as weighing 30 pounds. Bottom— Enchanting Oak Creek

There are no trees just around the schoolhouse, and at noon we all go down to a wide irrigation ditch bordered by trees to eat our luncheon. These children have never seen the ocean, and one who is over fourteen has never seen a train!

The youngsters already have brought us flowers and great luscious pears, huge Bartlett pears.

Mr. Girdner is progressive and earnest and kindly. His family do such things as regularly reading aloud together or all studying the science of music or the Palmer System of writing together in the evenings. I'm very glad I brought so many books.

Friday a.m. off for school, warm morning.

Much love to you all, Elsie

Shadyvale Ranch Cornville, Arizona
Yavapai County
Thursday Evening, September 18

Dear Mama and Aunt Mamie:

Mail came to us this morning before school that reached Cornville post office yesterday. I was very glad to have your belated letter and also your card, Mama. I hate to ask for so many things, "but feel as if we were out of the world here," and I keep thinking of things I particularly want. My Sears catalog came today, so we'll be sending to them. Please send things parcel post here if you can. I sent Paddy a card asking for burlap. It needn't be just Copenhagen blue, of course, but I meant a dull blue, probably not so dark as navy blue. We want it for draperies. I'll send a check later. Will that be all right? Well, I may put one in with this. I'd like an aluminum or granite cup or two.

We are in our new little house. The cloth ceiling (regular roof above that) is calcimined light blue, and new wallpaper is pretty blue. We aren't entirely settled yet, but are getting on well with our own breakfasts and luncheons. School children bring us eggs and butter, and the Girdners let us have melons, fruit and tomatoes, fine things free. They sell us good milk. So, we don't need much else. Mrs. Girdner serves us good dinners. Thank you for the pea soup.

Please excuse the way I write. For some time I may usually write so fast as to write badly. Wouldn't you rather have longer letters not so well written than shorter ones that had beautiful writing? Tonight I stayed at school until after six, working further over the new textbooks, etc. I've made some interesting preparations for my work tonight. As soon as I got home this afternoon, Marguerite and I donned old clothes and hurried to the creek for a bath before our six forty-five dinner. She had come home a little earlier than I tonight. It was hot today. The mornings are getting cooler, and the water felt perfectly scrumptious. Wish you could have seen us! We'll have to take a Kodak next time. I wore my pink crepe for a bathing suit (took it half off in the water as underclothes were beneath the bathing suit) and lay on my back on the rocks. The stream is swift and strong. It was great fun.

Last night we had a scare that proved to be nothing. About ten or after, long after the Girdners had gone to bed, I heard light footsteps, near our little house in their yard, and then someone turned the knob of our door. Marguerite had gone straight to sleep, and I'd been sitting on the edge of the bed, light out, too sleepy to roll in. The door was just beside me, so I knelt down quickly by it and leaned against it, though it was locked. While I softly woke Marguerite by pulling her sleeve, someone tried again to get in. I looked through the key hole, but couldn't tell in the bright moonlight whether I saw anything or not. We huddled on the bed, talking in whispers and scared to death. I wondered about all sorts of explanations, for I couldn't see how a sane burglar would run up so lightly and try so naturally to walk in with no signs of stealth. When I woke Marguerite, we both called out to know who was there, but there was no answer. We didn't like to wake the house, and were afraid to go near the windows. Finally, we decided we ought to call, so we shrieked wildly. Mr. Girdner answered immediately. He woke like a flash and told us to keep guard from the windows while he came down. He was with us in a jiffy, and we were all so frightened! Mrs. Girdner and Stanley and Eva soon followed, and pretty soon I was so relieved I didn't know what to do. Stanley had done it in his sleep. He is fond of us and had come over almost countless times bringing loads of

Cornville School 1913

things for us, armfuls from my trunk. Mrs. Girdner remembered seeing him go in or out of the room, and he remembered, as in a dream, finding himself here, or what must have been here, and finding himself going back into the house. He said he'd tie himself down tonight! We'd been so frightened that they were afraid we'd be nervous for a while, though they say this is a wonderfully safe locality. The dog is tied to the tree by our "cabin" now, and the older boys, who sleep out of doors in a canvas covered bed, like a schooner wagon, are going to move their bed near us. It seems very funny now.[1]

The schoolchildren are dear. They bring us fruit and flowers, etc. I have eighteen enrolled now, but have fifth grade (four of that number)

---

1   Stanley Girdner described their beds as being made from corn shucks. Eva and her mother had feather mattresses brought from Kansas. Eva described this covered wagon as a homemade bed, a box on legs. They used wagon bows, hardwood bent in a U shape and fastened to the bed frame and covered with canvas. This bed was about fifty feet from "the shack" so as to make the city teachers feel more secure.

Elsie's school children

only a small part of the day after my small youngsters go. I have seven small boys in first and second grades who are just about the same size and all wear overalls. When they are all at the board I can't tell some of them apart from the backs of their light or almost white heads. But one of them is a Mexican and the cutest, most picturesque boy you can imagine. He's brown as he can be, with wonderful, long-lashed, great, shining eyes, very, very dark. His teeth are even and shining-white, and his smile is bewitching. Many of my children, boys and girls alike, go barefooted. I love two of my girls especially, Sarah Stuck and Lavina Topping, who aren't "common," like some of the youngsters. One can tell what kinds of families they have. I love them all anyway. Then there's one baby, one of my six year olds, who is so tiny she is ridiculous as a child at school. She's Della Smith, whose sister is Nellie Smith. I wish you could see her. She's so funny I nearly choke. It's great fun to have the little tots and a wonderful privilege to be able to give to them. I'll tell you more of our house later. I like it. I'm very glad Papa's cough is better. Aren't you coming to Arizona?

Much love to all, Elsie
P.S. I forgot to tell you how well it agrees with my health here! I feel wonderfully and can do so much now.

Sept. 23, Tue. Noon, school.

Dear Family:

It is so cold today that the children are eating in the house. It certainly is an absolute change. It is windy and cloudy. Rained hard this morning before school.

I have 21 children enrolled now, but I don't have all of them at once. The fifth grade have their most important work with me, but stay in M's room most of the day and have part of their work with her. There are only four or five of them. I have nine in the Primer and First grade. My half Indian and my Mexican are both first graders and seem to be enemies. In general, the children are beautifully peaceful and seem very fond of each other. This morning they acted out the story of Cinderella, and that amused them so much it was hard to calm them down at all. Dramatization is supposed to be a regular part of first grade work. I certainly enjoy being near children.

We had quite an adventure coming home from our drive Sunday. We had walked a good part of the way to the cliff where the ruins are, going thru meadows and once all wading the creek. Glen Girdner went to the Post Office with the wagon and then drove back along the creek to meet us. We all got in the heavy farm wagon and Glen started across the creek where there were no tracks. He got into quicksand and the horses sank so that they were deep in. We jumped out and got to shore without trouble as the quicksand around here is not dangerous for people. Mrs. Girdner told us to stop to take off our shoes, but I didn't know then how mild the quicksand is about Cornville. I hardly think the shoes are ruined however!

I had worn my white ones to be more comfortable, not knowing what was ahead of me! They got out horses and wagon safely.

It is now four in the afternoon and the children are going. Oh, I wish you could see my long lines of boys at the blackboard, when the first and second grade are there, all looking so much alike in their overalls! My third and fourth grade pupils are all girls, and also my fifth grade. I certainly enjoy the work, but I am busy.

We get along well with our housekeeping arrangements. We have peanut butter, olives, nuts, little cakes, crackers and some canned things on hand. The Girdner children constantly bring fresh fruit and melons to our door. The milk I get from the Girdners is very good, and we get eggs thru the school children.

One of my very little boys has just ridden off in chaps. He looks so cunning!

The wallpaper I enclose is like that on our walls, freshly put there. Mrs. G. gave me what was leftover to use for scrapbook covers for the children to make. I'm going to use it to cover a waste-paper basket that I'm going to make out of cardboard for my schoolroom, while the children make little ones for their Art or busy work. My model will be the folding one I brot, which is very useful.

Stanley put up shelves for us over our two low windows. On the one over our library and dining table we have our books. Over the other window is our row of groceries that our china closet (made of a box) won't hold. Our washstand is also a box with shelves. It has legs, and the china closet is fastened high so that both are convenient. We have a good dresser with a large mirror, and I have all the drawers. Marguerite's trunk has splendid drawers. My trunk is left in the big house with things stored in it. We have a stove that I think will be good for heating and some cooking. It isn't a cooking stove and has no oven. We have a large wardrobe made out of boards in one corner, with a curtain before it. The cloth ceiling is calcimined light blue but we can still see thru it in certain lights and see the beams of the roof. The roof is tin and the rain on it sounds loud. When we get our blue curtains we will really be quite cozy. We want them for the wash-stand, china closet, and windows, and perhaps for a screen. The room looks pleasant to me, with its books and familiar pictures, and the lovely views of trees and hills from the windows. My Mt. Baldy picture I particularly enjoy.

All my things came safely. Thank you again for your help in packing, Aunt Mamie!

Mrs. Girdner certainly is a fine woman. I admire Mr. Girdner very much, too. Their children are all dears. Any little thing charms little Eva. Last night I heard her wish for a little pencil and gave her a tiny one (like those on tally-cards) from my trunk. She was perfectly delighted. They are all more than kind to us.

I've received a fine lot of mail from a lot of people. My Pageant book has come and is splendid. I love my home letters.

Alice, I'll subscribe for the Pomona College Student Life magazine and then send the copies on to you, where you may keep them. Does that suit you? The news wouldn't be very old by the time it would reach you.

If you make up your minds, even only half-way, about a trip to Arizona, please let me know! Did I tell you that we'll probably go to Teachers Institute either the last of October or first part of November in Prescott or Phoenix, while our salary goes on? I suppose we shall be gone at least a week.

Now it is almost five P.M. and I'm going home, and will try to get some fresh air before dinner.

Little Sarah will mail this for me today, so it will leave Cornville tomorrow.

> With Much Love to All, Elsie
> P.S. I think the heat was good
> for me, but this cold weather
> makes me feel "fine!"

2

Social Life to Dawn

"Convent isolation of two and a half months still unbroken, no foreboding that social life is to dawn on the morrow."

Writing letters provided Elsie with an important link to home. She wrote often and tried to give her family a picture of country life in Arizona. The post office was three miles from the Girdner farm, and the teachers often enjoyed a walk there. Twice a week the mail was delivered in a cloth sack to a mailbox only one-half mile away. It was the mailbox for several families in that area, and each sack bore the name of the ranch or family. Elsie watched with fascination one day as young Eva put her ear on a big limestone rock beside the mailbox and exclaimed, "He's coming!" She could hear the rumble of the wagon wheels through the hollow underground spaces in the limestone. Arizona was teaching this teacher a number of things.

Elsie must have been satisfied as she thought of these first weeks in Arizona. The schoolhouse was the center of community life in this isolated area. It was the only place for "ditch meetings," which were held to decide the use of creek water. (Oak Creek settlement was about ten miles long with ranches on both sides of the creek, and there were about twenty miles of ditches providing water for some thirty ranches.) The drab wooden structure also served as the site for occasional dances and Sunday school. Isolated Cornville was not visited by the circuit-riding preachers, so there was only Sunday school for the children, where Elsie found herself playing the old organ.

Ordering groceries, clothing, and school supplies from a catalog was a nuisance as it was difficult to know if the color or size would be correct. Elsie had often said she liked any color "as long as it's blue," so she'd order blue and hope for the best. Canned goods had to be ordered since there was no refrigeration and no ice was available for an icebox. If a farmer butchered a cow, he would have to sell and deliver the beef immediately to his neighbors, who would have to use it right away or dry it as jerky. Pork sausage was preserved by frying the spicy patties and storing them between layers of fat in a bucket. Old sheets were torn into narrow strips and used to create a bag into which the sausage was tightly stuffed. Fresh milk from the Girdners' cow would sour overnight if kept in the "western cooler" (a wooden-framed, burlap-covered structure over which water was poured to allow a breeze to cool the contents).

The girls spent much of their time outdoors. Sometimes school was held under the bright blue sky or in the shade of a tree. The children would sit on rocks, boards, or damaged shingles that had been discarded by the men of the school district when they added a porch roof around the building. The shingles also served as toy gun materials and as shovels to dig up the wild sego lilies, which the children loved to eat. Elsie was amazed as she watched them eating the lily bulbs. Apparently, these barefoot children thrived on the air, sunshine, dirt, and sego lily bulbs!

Elsie also thrived on this outdoor living, especially as she began to spend many lovely hours beside the creek. She had never been seriously ill but was considered delicate and perhaps frail, and the pure Arizona air and sunshine seemed to have a tonic effect on her health. (For years doctors had been sending their tuberculosis patients and invalids to Arizona to recover.) The creek was the most soothing place she had ever been. It lightened her loneliness, eased the problems at school, and provided the most perfect, private, quiet place to read. Long ago she had discovered that reading was for her almost as necessary to life as breathing. There was one large, graceful old sycamore whose roots seemed to be built for Elsie, and she would relax and read there almost daily. Sometimes she would read aloud to Eva or Marguerite, for Elsie loved the sound of words almost as much as their meaning.

Elsie had begun to joke about their "convent isolation." The employment agency had told the girls that the very best locations to find husbands were Arizona and Alaska. Elsie had assured them she was going only to teach, not to look for a husband. But she did miss the company of other people her own age. Excitement arrived the day she discovered a message written in Latin on her chalkboard after school. In English it read, "I came, I saw, I conquered." Elsie decided that the young man teaching at the Red Rock School, almost fifteen miles away, must be the mysterious writer. There was nobody in Cornville who knew Latin! Soon Eugene Barron, the Red Rock Latin teacher and his cowboy friend Fritz Schuerman came to invite the teachers to a dance. Elsie and Marguerite became acquainted with several young cowboys that night. Perhaps not surprisingly, the "convent isolation" for the two attractive young schoolteachers ended the night of this first dance.

Cornville, Arizona
Sunday, Oct. 19, 1913

Dearest Papa,

I've been waiting to write to you separately before, but have kept sending family letters. I can't write much tonight, for I must go to bed early The

33

day seemed full. Sunday school usually begins late and takes a good part of the morning. I played the organ again today. After Sunday school some young boys and a man who was coming to the Girdners' to dinner hung around outside our cabin and talked with us while we sat on the doorstep. It was about three when we settled down after dinner. I took a rest. We always have Chicken on Sunday, usually no meat other days unless bacon.

It took quite a while to read our mail this afternoon. I was glad to have Mama's card written the 16th. I had my <u>Student Life</u> too, and letters from Alice Parker.

My payment to Mrs. Girdner for the first four weeks after we came into the cabin was only $11.75 for room rent, dinners, and milk. We save a good deal by doing so much of our own work. We are very busy on Saturday mornings cleaning house, etc. Yesterday I spent a long time ironing and mending, too.

This pen certainly is abominable!

Late this afternoon I went for a walk with the children. The trees by the creek are turning yellow, and are very beautiful. The ash and sycamore look especially like autumn. Yellow masses of thick wild grapevines are wonderful.

We expect to go to Prescott a week from tomorrow for Institute. Institute is Tuesday, Wednesday, and Thursday, the 28th, 29th, and 30th. I am going to visit Laura Kent instead of having to go to a hotel. Isn't that lovely? It will be good to see a friend in this strange land! We expect to get someone to take us to Jerome early enough to get a noon train for Prescott. If we went by stage we'd have to go Saturday and stay overnight in Jerome.

The Northern Arizona fair is to be in progress, and I think will be interesting.[2] There are soldiers stationed at Prescott.

---

2   "In 1913 most of the residents of Arizona had never seen one of those new-fangled airplanes until they attended the first Northern Arizona State Fair. The Yavapai County Chamber of Commerce laid out a racetrack, erected buildings and a grandstand. The Santa Fe railroad ran special passenger trains from the downtown depot to the fair grounds for a fare of fifteen-cents a round trip. Governor Hunt and his staff occupied the officials box during the opening ceremonies and Tom Mix, Director of Events, put on a dazzling display of horsemanship and trick riding to the crowd's delight but the special feature attraction everyone waited in anticipation for was the sky-borne arrival of an airplane. 'Here it comes, here it comes!' the

I may stay over until Saturday or early Sunday, getting the Sunday stage to Cornville. Probably that will be about the only way to arrange it.

I hope you are well and that real estate is prospering.

With much love to you and
all the family, Elsie

Tuesday, Nov. 18, 1913

Dearest Papa:

I was certainly glad to have a letter from you.

The weather has been cloudy and rainy by fits and starts for days and days. They say that is very unusual here. I go for walks anyway, and enjoy them very much. The scenery is truly autumnal now, with the trees yellow or bare, and leaves over the ground. It is beautiful. Friday after school we drove to the post office in the big farm wagon with one of the boys. Saturday we explored again some very interesting old caves in cliffs nearby, where the Indians once lived. Sunday we had our walk to the post office. We had to go the long way over the mesa to avoid some of the creek crossings, and still further to avoid an impassable ditch. Then we lost the way, so that it was almost dark when we got to the curve of the creek before the post office. We had been walking two hours! Doris Johnson, one of my fifth grade girls, lives near there. Her people have several times wanted us to come see them for all day or overnight. Her father saw us across the creek, and came over for us with a horse on which we both rode over at once, bareback! We had a pleasant supper with them, for they made us stay, and then Mr. Johnson brought us home horseback. Marguerite rode on the saddle then, and I sat behind the saddle all the way! It was all fun. I go for walks after school, too, so you see that I get a good deal of exercise and fresh air.

Journal Miner reported of the crowd's reaction when aviator L. F. Nixon hove into sight in his Curtis bi-plane. Nixon piloted his air bird to an astounding height of 1,000 feet and circled the fairgrounds twice before returning to terra firma. Several years later Tom Mix was one of the highest paid movie stars." (Sharlot Hall Museum Past Days article, September 30, 2001).

After our screen door was put on, we had the other door open at night—but now the screen one is too swollen with dampness to close. We have the windows wide open at night. We have physical exercises in my room at school, and hope soon to have some of the regular school work out-of-doors. I have 23 children now, besides the fifth grade.

The Girdners' peaches have just gone. We always had plenty in our shack. Now we particularly appreciate the gifts of apples from the children at school.

With much love, Elsie

Elsie's Diary

First Diary Entry for 1913

Nov. 20, 1913, Thurs. Cornville Arizona. Convent isolation of two and a half months still unbroken, no foreboding that social life is to dawn on the morrow.

Nov. 21, Fri. Went with Gene and George Moore and Marguerite to a dance at the schoolhouse. Danced most with Mr. Hancock. Got acquainted with

Mr. Hurst (who, as well as George Moore asked me for the Red Rock dance).

Nov. 23, Sun. Went to Sunday school. Talked with Mrs. Girdner about the dance. Mr. Hurst called and stayed to tea. Mr. Hancock called. Two more bids for the Red Rock dance refused.[3]

Nov. 24, Mon. School as usual. Note on the door from Karl Hurst!

Nov. 25, Tues. School. Mr. Hurst and Mr. Ferguson spent the evening. Convent isolation forgotten. Kodak mended.

Nov. 26, Wed. Explored caves with children. My room gave a Thanksgiving program before Marguerite's room. Lizzie kept me laughing! Read Browning and Shakespeare to Marguerite.

Nov. 27, Thurs. Thanksgiving Day. Waked by Karl! Marguerite and I walked to Mrs. Hurst's with Myrlie in 1-1/4 hours. Beautiful! Croquet and dinner with Edna and Harriet. Fergie and Karl brought us home. Mr. Hancock called.

Nov. 28, 1913 Friday

Dearest Mother,

Such a funny week this has been, after our entire isolation that I wrote you about on Sunday. Tuesday evening Karl Hurst and his friend Mr. Ferguson, who is interested in Marguerite, called. Mr. Hurst brought a box of apples, and the other man brought candy. Wednesday evening I was reading Browning and Shakespeare aloud to M. while she embroidered, because the next day was to be a holiday. Mr. Hurst came to the door before we were up Thanksgiving Day wanting to see me about the trip for tomorrow. We ironed

---

3   Mrs. Girdner, looking very bothered and embarrassed, had come to the teachers and reminded them that their recommendation had said that they were good Christian girls. She explained that they had understood that the teachers would not attend these local dances mainly because liquor was always present. The children admired their teachers and their attendance might influence the children to think that drunken behavior was acceptable. Elsie thought the mother appeared almost sick with worry and she assured her that they would not go to any future dances if that was how she felt. She noticed the flash of anger in Marguerite's face. There was no way Marguerite could attend if Elsie was not going.

a little and I went to the box on the hill for the mail. I certainly was glad to have Aunt Mamie's card. Alice's bundle came, too. Thank her for me. Did she make the turkey game for me? It will be splendid to have for the children for rainy recesses, and is so well done.

We left home about a quarter to one, and got to the Hursts' just about two, the hour set for dinner. It was a glorious walk! The air was crisp but the sun bright. We went over the hills and then by the winding creek where there were leaves under our feet and golden ones on the cottonwoods over our heads.

The Hursts call their place Sycamore. It has beautiful big sycamores all about it, and a huge, thick, green lawn, the first lawn I've set my feet upon in three months, I believe. The creek flows in front, and the hills are all about. I was very glad to be able to imagine you all as at Riverside. I hope you had a splendid time. I thought a lot about you yesterday. The Hurst family consists of Mr. Hurst, looking like a typical country gentleman[4]; Mrs. H, who is large and jolly, with a fine, good face and beautiful, sincere friendliness; Ruth, aged 13, not strong enough to be in school this year; and two beautiful, adorable little girls of 3 and 4 years, about the dearest tots I've ever seen. The son Karl lives on his own ranch half a mile away. He came to dinner and so did Mr. Ferguson.

It was all lovely, looked more like home than anything else I've seen in Cornville. The living room is simple and artistic, and they have a piano, magazines, and sheet music. The napkins and shining silver surely looked good to us on the dinner table! We had a feast, huge, fine turkey, delicious mashed potato (unlike any other we've had lately), two salads, celery, cabbage, coffee, punch, floating island, angel's food cake, mince and pumpkin pie, and nuts. We played croquet on that beautiful lawn, romped with the children and enjoyed all the day. Karl Hurst and Mr. Ferguson brought us home in a two-seated "rig" with two horses; that is a big improvement on the farm wagon we are used to. They stayed quite awhile

---

4   *Yavapai Monthly* magazine for January 15, 1915, reported that, "J. O. Hurst is one of the remarkable successful orchardists of the Verde. His apples, peaches and plums have won prizes at numerous exhibitions."

and then the "Kentuckian" called before they left at 7:30.

K. H. is going to bring a chicken and bread to us this afternoon. We are going to fry it and make sandwiches for tomorrow. He asked me if I wanted Marguerite and Mr. F. to go, and of course I did. We're going to drive to Montezuma's Well, a famous place throughout Arizona. We've wanted to see it for a long time.

Tonight I hope I'll have a letter from home, because of Christmas I seem to keep asking for things. I should like about six simple holly-covered, pasteboard boxes sent me, about 3 inches square, to send some inexpensive little gifts in.

Karl Hurst

Very much love to you, and to all, Elsie

Nov. 28, Fri. Karl Hurst brought a chicken and I fried it while Marguerite made cake. Sandwiches and late hours!

Nov. 29, Sat. Drove to Montezuma's well. Marguerite, Karl, Fergie and I, a 30 mile trip. Cold and sunshine. Marvelous place. Rowing, caves, climb to ruins, luncheon and ferns. "First star I see tonight!"[5]

Nov. 30, Sun. Sunday at Cornville. Sunday school. Letters. Walk.

---

5   Elsie elaborated on this memorable trip, explaining how they ascended the barren hillside and suddenly there before them were the cool, clear, sunken lake and Indian homes in the surrounding cliffs. The young men had brought a lantern to explore the cold, pitch-black caves that had once been Indian dwellings. Once inside, the men mischievously extinguished the lamp on purpose. She described how she felt genuine terror as they teased about not having matches and being trapped forever in this cave. Soon matches were revealed and the terror disappeared as the lamp was relit. Rowing on the lake soothed the nerves of the girls. Elsie delighted in discovering pieces of Indian pottery and luscious, deep-green ferns that grew alongside the irrigation ditches that radiated from the well. Riding back in the cold, open farm wagon she wished upon the "first star" as it appeared in the moonlit sky.

Dec. 1, Mon. School, Snow! Played at snow-balling at recess. Read <u>At the End of the Rainbow</u> by Gene Stratton Porter.

Dec. 2, Tues. Karl Hurst called.

Dec. 3, Wed. After school went horseback to the Post Office with Karl. Late dinner for two at the Girdners'.

Dec. 4, Thurs. School. Exciting note found on the door at noon.

Dec. 7, Sun. Read <u>Friendship Village Love Stories</u> aloud. Fergie and Marguerite and I walked by the creek. Karl arrived! Tea for four. Moonlight walk. Jerome lights. [Sometimes at night the girls sat by the creek and watched the lights of Jerome up on the hillside. The smelter at Jerome provided a spectacular nighttime sight. Large amounts of molten slag were poured over the hillside, and the view from Oak Creek was sometimes like watching the glow of a faraway volcano.]

December 8, Monday

Dearest Mother,

Again I didn't write on Sunday. After Sunday school we got our house in order, had dinner and I rested and read. Then Karl Hurst and Mr. Ferguson came to supper, and it was late when they left. Saturday I saw to some Christmas things and did some washing and rested and read a little.

For supper last night we had quite a little spread. Marguerite made cheese "dream cakes" on the chafing dish and I creamed oysters and served them on toasted crackers. The others had coffee. The G.'s had given us fresh radishes and celery. We had pineapple and little cakes (out of a box) and some after dinner mints M.'s mother had sent her, and later we had some of Karl's apples. The boys certainly have brought us a lot of candy.

They cut cards to see who would do dishes, and the lot fell to Karl and me. The others went for a moonlight stroll and so did we after awhile. Next Sunday after Sunday school and lunch Karl is to take me horseback to the mouth of Oak Creek where there are Indian ruins.

If you won't tell outside the family (and of course that includes Ernest), I'll tell you that Karl is, or thinks he is desperately in love with me already. He thinks himself that it seems silly when he's only known me two weeks, but he remarked in a note that nevertheless, "facts remain the same!" He wrote the note to tell me that he better not come to see me anymore, since however hard he tried in the end I'd be sure to go back to California. He's decided now to come anyway, which seems more sensible. He feels so bad about it that I'm terribly sorry for him. I hope he'll succeed in trying to feel like just a friend instead, for I don't believe I'd care enough for any man to marry him unless he cared as much as I about books!

Karl has been to school so little that he's a perfect marvel to be so well-educated. He's not a bit like the usual cowboys about here, tho he was a cowboy for 5 years. He's elegant and they're not! He's very fine and splendid, and I like him ever so much. We are very congenial in many ways. I think he must be the "goodest" man I've ever known at all besides Papa! He reminds me somewhat of Bill Brewster [Pomona College friend] in his love of the out-of-doors and rather by contrast, tho with some points in common, he makes me think of Charles Stearns. [Charles Stearns was Professor of Biblical History and Literature at Pomona College.] I certainly have been appreciating him as a friend, as he's more "my kind" than anyone else I know here. Marguerite is too worldly to be very congenial to me. Karl has been over almost every day in these two weeks.

Next Saturday we expect two other men to lunch, the Red Rock school teacher, who invited himself and a cowboy friend. Mr. Barron, the teacher, is gay and rather interesting. He's called on us before you know.

Mrs. Hurst, Karl's mother, who asked us for Thanksgiving sent a note inviting me to have Christmas dinner with them. That will be more like home than any other place where I could be for Christmas in Cornville, and I am glad I'm going. Karl has asked to drive me over, it's three miles.

I've been playing the awful old organ in Sunday school quite regularly lately.

I'm busy with plans for the Christmas Eve entertainment.

Very Much Love to you all, My
precious family, Elsie

Dec. 10, Wed. Marguerite and I hunted mistletoe by the creek. Karl brought the mail and found us.

Dec. 11, Thurs. Children at work on Christmas decorations and entertainment in earnest.

Dec. 12, Fri. Reymundo, Jessie D, Doris and Karl at the shack after school. Karl and I watched the moonlight brighten on the creek, and got supper together.

Dec. 13, Sat. Gave a luncheon to Mr. Barron and Fritz Schuerman of Red Rock. Walked by the creek. Mr. Hancock spent ALL the evening.

Karl and Elsie

Dec. 14, Sun. Sunday school. Karl and I rode horse back to the cliff dwellers ruins at the mouth of Oak Creek, 10 mile trip. "If" poem of Browning's![6] Rained. Tea at home for four. Read poetry to Karl, Tennyson.

Dec.1 6, Tues. Returned from dinner to find two men quite at home in the shack.

Letter from Elsie's mother
Long Beach
December 14, 1913

My Dear Elsie,

Your letter to Hylinda and me came yesterday. I hope you have had a good rest today. I am afraid Mr. Hurst intrudes too much on your time for rest. His must have been a case of "love at first sight," for sure! From

---

6   Elsie may have been referring to Elizabeth Barrett Browning's *Sonnets from the Portuguese*: "If thou must love me, let it be for naught. Except for love's sake only . . ."

all you say he must be a fine young man, and if his not loving books as well as you were the only drawback, I should not suppose that need to keep you from marrying him, but I should be afraid that the life of a farmer's wife would be too hard and uncongenial for you. I should like to see all of you girls married to good men. I believe it is right to marry, if you are <u>very</u> <u>sure</u> the man is the right one!

Hylinda seems to think she may teach in the Chinese mission—a mission in Los Angeles for immigrant children—and also get tutoring at night for Chinese young men who work during the day.

Very Much Love, Mama

Letter from Elsie's father
Long Beach Dec. 14, 1913

Dear Elsie

You write good letters and we are glad to get them so often and hear just how you are getting on. I am sorry you will not be home Christmas but owing to the time it takes and the expense I think you are wise in not coming as you would not get much rest. That we shall miss you goes without saying. You will have a good chance to rest and read and from all accounts you will not have a very dull time.

I don't suppose you take that young man very seriously. You ought to know a young man a long time, something about his past life, habits etc., as well as about his prospects and industry and congeniality, before you take him seriously. I believe in love and marriage but it is a serious thing to consider. I would like to see you married to a sincere Christian.

It rained last night and this a.m. as I had a cold I did not go to church, it is clear this evening and Mama and I are the only ones at home. I am very glad you are feeling so well. Mrs. Rankin read me part of a letter from their bunch in which she said you were well thought of in the school.

I wish we could go to Arizona if it was not so far away, we have not decided yet about going to the foothills, if I was sure it would be best for

Mama's health and mine I would try hard to go. We have been considering a trade near Perris for our Pomona and Claremont property, have not decided yet.

I hope you will have a good Christmas and will continue well and happy,

Lovingly, Papa
Sweet One—just a little corner for me
to say how much I love you—Aunt Mamie

Cornville, Arizona
December 18, 1913

Dearest Family,

This is to wish you all a Merry Christmas! How I should like to be with you! I hope you will enjoy the day in every way, be sure not to miss me too much! I seem to be getting very husky. That's a good Christmas gift. [For years Elsie struggled to weigh more than 100 pounds.]

Karl drove me to the post office after school tonight, and I sent a little package addressed to Mama. Marguerite will take this tomorrow and mail it somewhere, and you'll very likely get it before the package. I do hope the things I've sent to the rest of you indirectly will be there on time.

My vacation has begun! I know I'll miss M., but I'll surely be busy. I have loads of laundry work to do, and would like to do some housecleaning.

Monday Karl and I are going out for trees and greens, Tuesday the afternoon will be filled by a dress rehearsal of the youngsters, and Wednesday there will be the decorating and trimming of the trees, etc. That night I surely will have enough to do! I'll put in one of the programs later. I'll tell you more about it. I wrote several of the things my children have, and M. thought out the Toy Shop stunt her children have, where each represents a doll wound up, a bit like Mrs. Jarley's wax works.

Christmas you know I'm to be at the Hursts'. Probably dinner will be very late, and I'll have a morning here first. Tonight I mustn't write much, because it's my first chance to go to bed early. Wrapping up of packages and writing Christmas cards and notes has taken time other nights, as has

Karl! Last night he had dinner with us at the Girdners', who insisted on his coming. They like him. Then Fergie came and took M. to the post office on Karl's horse. Karl and I had a long visit as a consequence. The poor man is "hard hit," as they say, I certainly enjoy being with him. He's a year or so younger than I, but seems much older. He's certainly interesting, and it's delightful to have somebody near in the country that is really congenial. I enjoy Fergie, too.

Your lovely letters, Papa's, Mama's, Aunt Mamie's, came tonight. The cards are beautiful. Thank you Paddy Dear. I enjoyed all the letters very much. This is to you all, the whole five of you. And of course I send love to Ernest. I send my love to Frisk, too. How is he? Aunt Mamie, I suppose your Eastern packages have been pouring in. Hylinda, I hope you can have work in the Chinese school. I got the book I've sent you because of what I've heard of the author, and thought you'd like it, and I wanted to read it myself, too. So I read it first, and I think it is splendid. I hope you will care for it.

Papa, I do hope your cold will be entirely gone by Christmas.
Marguerite's children made the programs.

Marguerite will try to long distance you some day while she is home. She'll ask for you, Mama. I just thought you'd like to talk with her because we've been living together. I've grown very fond of her. She'll be home from about noon Sunday to Friday.

I'll think of you all heaps on Christmas.

My dear love to each and
every one of you, Elsie

Dec. 18, Thurs. Karl came to the Girdners' for dinner. Marguerite and Fergie rode to the post office later, while Karl and I kept the fire. Finished reading Washington Gladden's <u>Being a Christian</u>.

Dec. 19, Fri. Karl and I drove to the post office.

Dec. 20, Sat. Rose at 4:30 A.M. to see Marguerite leave for California. Walked and cleaned house. Karl called, spent the evening.

Dec. 21, Sun. At four went to the beautiful Bog—saw wild violets, columbines, Indian paintbrushes, Mariposa lilies, ferns. Pancakes fried in the stove for two.

Dec. 22, Mon. Karl and I drove over 20 miles to Dry Creek, Red Rock region. Red rocks and giant evergreens, brought home 5 Christmas trees. Costumes, etc.

Dec. 23, Tues. Final rehearsal. Children in the shack stringing popcorn.

Dec. 24, Wed. Christmas Eve. Decorated all day, tore from 8:45 A.M. to 11 P.M., then I was stage manager in the evening. Tree and children a joy. Then Karl and the fire!

Dec. 25, Thurs. Christmas Day. Letters and packages around my tree and a stocking. Dinner at the Hursts', drive with Karl. The Girdners came to a candy feed.

Dec. 26, Fri. Recuperation and letters. Walk with Eva over the hills. More gifts. A long, fond farewell. Curtain.

3

Wrestling with Fate

"Fire by the creek and moonlight. Then Karl and I wrestled with fate for hours. Glasses broken."

It must have been difficult for Elsie to say good night to Karl that day after Christmas in 1913. Perhaps she felt that the curtain had closed on their relationship as in the final act of a play as he announced to her his intention to stay away for a few weeks. It seems he was trying to protect his own heart in this distancing. Elsie herself was probably afraid to admit to her parents that this cowboy so intent on winning her love was actually only twenty-one years old, while she was twenty-five. Despite his youth, Karl had accomplished much and had already acquired his own farm. Elsie was comfortable with Karl and their friendship, but she was not ready to call it love.

Elsie had arrived in Cornville feeling a bit superior to these poorly educated "back woods" ranchers and cattlemen. Years later, in her taped story of this time, she referred to herself as a "bit of a snob." But slowly this feeling was transformed to admiration and respect, and perhaps even envy. She had read *Adventures in Contentment* and *Laddie* while sitting on the banks of Oak Creek. She wrote that these made her want to marry a farmer. This rugged, beautiful Verde Valley in Arizona was "hard living," but men who had chosen this hard life seemed to possess some qualities not present in the city-bred university men Elsie had known in college. She could not help but compare Arizonans to some of the wealthy, intellectual, college-educated people who had been a part of her life in California. She could not picture most of them being able to cope or thrive without electricity, running water, automobiles, and grocery stores.

Her father was unusual in that he was a blend of city man and farmer, selling real estate each fall and winter and growing apples on the mountain each summer. They were like two different worlds, the modern city life and the isolated country life that was so simple and uncluttered, yet hard. There was for Elsie a tie to both. In college she had thrived on the plays, concerts, and literary clubs, and she missed those. Even so, the creek with its soothing, enchanting sounds and smells, and the beautiful trees and hills surrounding it were like a newfound discovery to her. Marguerite could not wait to return to the modern fast-paced world. Elsie seemed to want both worlds. Her modern knight would have to be a "cultured cowboy."

Cornville
Friday, Dec. 26, 1913

My very dear Family,

What a splendid Christmas you sent me! I don't know how to thank you for all the lovely things, which certainly are just what I wanted! They all came, 3 boxes, with a delightful lot of other things for me, on Christmas Eve. They were in very good condition. Karl helped me open the two big boxes that night, because I couldn't wait until morning for everything. The things to eat you made yourself are too good for words, Mama, and it is lovely to have them from home. The fruitcake I'll keep awhile. The cookies are a joy, and the candies all delicious. The coconut candy is awfully good, Alice. And that fat home-like stocking, Aunt Mamie! I let out such a shriek when that came to view Karl must have thought me an infant! Before I went to bed I put on my table the lovely wee evergreen Karl got for me when we went for the big trees, and piled my packages all around it high, and tied my unlooked at stocking to my little bedpost! It was fearfully late then and I didn't get up until ten on Christmas. I made my fire, and then went back to bed to look at my stocking, just as I would have seen it first at home. I did think a great deal of everyone of you, with very special love.

The candied cherries and the ginger I particularly appreciated in the stocking, Aunt Mamie. I'd been wishing for raisins and dates, too, Mama. All the candy from the Palm Sweet Shop "looked good to me." I'm having a feast of candy that will last a long time, and it's delightful to have so much that I can give it out freely to some of these people who don't know so much about candy! Someone else here, I think it must have been Mrs. Hurst, gave me a box of delicious homemade candy. There was a dainty cup and saucer from "the children." M. and I got a fussy card of greeting from Mr. Barron, the Red Rock school teacher. Glen Girdner gave me an ancient Indian war-club, head of stone that he said I could give the Pomona museum. I'm charmed with that. Mrs. G. made a pretty towel rack for M. and me. I know I'll have at least cards from several more of my friends. It's almost worthwhile being "away" to be so beautifully remembered.

Mrs. G. told me she had written you a Christmas letter, Mama. From the way she spoke, I wondered if possibly she wrote partly to speak of Karl. She likes him ever so much, and praise from her seems to be mighty hard to win. Do please tell me if she says anything about him! Possibly she thinks he stays too late when he calls, or that we should oftener have a chaperon! But she's never intimated that. It would be hard to arrange anything conventionally in Arizona.

The entertainment went off beautifully, and I did enjoy it all, work and all. May I be so immodest as to remark that I had to boss everything (at least I did and was expected to), decorations, etc., as well as program, and that I seem to have pleased the neighborhood? Mrs. G. worked like a Trojan, and so did the Johnsons and one or two other people. Mr. J. was a splendid Santa Claus.

Monday Karl and I drove some 20 miles there and back (was that shocking?) and got beautiful trees. The place was beautiful. One tree was on each side of the front space used as a platform. Tuesday there was a final rehearsal. Wednesday I tore from before nine A.M. until eleven or so at night, except for fifteen minutes when I lay down at noon, and a quiet time for my lunch. I got up about 11:30 today! It is glorious to be so well and able to do so much. I seem to thrive on everything now. This place and the change were very good for me apparently.

We decorated with garlands and wreaths and had large candles in the windows, and little ones on the tree.[7] M. and I got tree ornaments, tinsel, etc. for our share to help the Sunday school, and the children in my room made lots of gifts and decorations. It looked beautiful. We had gifts (M. and I) for the children, and the community gave money for a treat of nuts, candy, and oranges.

I wore my pink and black and white dainty dress tho I was behind one of the trees to prompt most of the time. My friends, the Hursts, Fergie, and so on were much amused by the glimpses they caught of the way the youngsters mobbed me with questions the whole evening. On every side

---

7   Elsie mail-ordered delicate, white, twisted candles that she placed by clips all over the tree. She must have wanted the school children to have an unforgettable memory of this Christmas. Seventy-five years later Eva Girdner Stone could still describe to me that tree from 1913.

it was, "When is Santa Claus coming, Miss Hayes? Miss Hayes, let me put this on the tree. Is Santa Claus going to bring me something? When is my piece? Who's going to dress me?" etc., etc., etc. My name sounded in my ears as constantly as the buzzing of bees.

Mrs. G. was costumer, and did it beautifully, while I helped a bit with that and acted as manager. The children were adorable! They looked so dear in their "best clothes," I wanted to hug them all to death. They did beautifully. I wrote one or two of the things.

We had garlands and so on to add to the effectiveness. I had to face the audience to lead the Santa Claus song at the end that was the signal to Santa himself to run in with his pack on his back. Since I know so little about music I felt like an idiot to go through with all the motions! But it seemed to be all right, as far as Cornville is a judge. It would be different in a town!

Afterward, when at last costumes etc. were collected, Karl and another young man and Glen carried my things to the shack. I surely was excited. Almost all my packages from home and all came in that day's mail, and were brought to the schoolhouse in the evening by the Johnson's.

I hardly had time to be homesick. That evening Karl stayed a long while after he made my fire, and the next day, Christmas, we didn't leave here for his mother's until after one, and yet I hadn't more than had time to look at my things before he came at twelve. I took little ten-cent gifts to the little Hurst girls, and that was lots of fun, glass watches with leather and fob, filled with Pure Food candy, from a California mail order house. We played croquet, Mr. Hurst, Fergie, Karl, and I, for Mrs. Hurst wouldn't let me help with the dinner. The children were a delight. They are the most beautiful little girls! I had a lovely time playing with them and looking at their new toys. The dinner: turkey, cranberry jelly, salted almonds, fruitcake, mince pie, and ever so many other things were like home. I like the family ever so much. Karl brought me home before dark and stayed a while, and then I got all the Girdners to come over for candy and to see my things. They are lovely to me. I showed them my entire photograph and Kodak book last night. Mrs. G. said it seemed as if she knew my folks and felt as if they were her friends. I hadn't known before she thought that much of me.

How I hope your Christmas was a happy, lovely one! I want to hear all about it. I hope you aren't tired out by all this letter. I hope my things got to you on time. I suppose from what you said of Uncle Ed's turkey that you had one on Christmas.

Thank you very much, Mama, for seeing to my pictures, and to so many other things. I hope Alice will have sent me some correspondence cards. You are a treasure, Alice. How is Ernest?

Glen is waiting longer than I had expected for his mother's letters, but I probably won't have time to read this over. He and some other schoolboy put the partition up again this morning, and then I helped them get things into order.

Karl is so funny! I like him immensely, but I hardly think I'll marry him! He thinks he hardly has a right to ask me because he hasn't been to school more, but he continues to ask me, just the same, over and over!!! He is a splendid man and such a contrast to the Cornville type that his good clothes and good looks alone might be enough to convince me, if I were different! He may stay away for a month, and perhaps he won't come anymore after that. He thinks it is too hard for him if there isn't a chance for him.

I'm brave now I'm well and have been staying alone all night. Eva is too much the "baby" to leave home at night. The boys sleep out and near the shack. The school year is half over.

> With very much love to you all,
> Always, Your Elsie

Dec. 27, 1913 Sat. Work, washed, ironed, mopped. Wrote letters.

Dec. 28, Sun. Lunched alone. Drove to Jerome with Karl for Marguerite—30 mile trip! Tea at the Robinson's. Glad to have the wanderer return.

Dec. 29, Mon. School week of vacation over. Life goes on as before. "Work is a boon!" School children come to see our gifts.

Dec. 30, Tues. Children after vacation act like "the morning after the night before." Ruth Hurst enters school, and I wonder. . . Still living on candy

Dec. 31, Wed. Party omitted; but Fergie had dinner with us, helped pop corn, and listened while I read <u>T.Tembarom</u> aloud until after the dawning of 1914. Tried to console me!

Jan. 1, 1914 Thurs. Oak Creek, New Years Day! School children called on me at noon in the shack. Poetry and candy for my room out-of-doors at 10 minutes of 4 in celebration.

Jan. 2, Fri. School. Shopped by mail, homesick?

Jan. 3, Sat. Mail good to have. Slept late. Cleaned house. Marguerite and I walked to Mrs. Hurst's, 3 miles.

Jan. 4, Sun. Sunday school. Elected teacher of primary class. Rode with Eva and brought back the mail. Read poems by Arnold.

Jan. 5, Mon. School went more smoothly than for some time, quieted down now. Rode with the girls, met Karl. He came to the shack for something to eat. Beautiful moonlight on the rocks!

Jan. 6, Tues. School with classes out-of-doors under the mesquite bushes. Read aloud from <u>T. Tembarom</u>.

Jan. 7, Wed. School. Tied a towel around Margaret's mouth! [At other times she made the children stand facing the wall as punishment.] M. and I rode to the post office with Doris and Jessie, and then bareback over the creek. Walked home. Fun!

Jan. 9, Fri. School. Karl and Fergie called, and again K. and I kept the fire, while M. fell from his horse! Then read to M. and F. and after midnight saw a comet!

Jan. 10, Sat. Rose late, walked to Mrs. Johnson's to call. Ramon took us over the creek! Walked home in the moonlight. Karl brought his petition for "Oak Creek."

Jan. 11, Sun. Walked to the dam with Karl; rode "Nig" to the post office. Then K. and F. really "called." A new unpleasantness arose and was mitigated.

Jan. 12, Mon. School and <u>T. Tembarom</u>.

Jan. 13, Tues. School, washed, saw how my book ended!

Elsie's "Kodak" drawn by great grandson Dan Waite

Jan. 14, Wed. "Scraps" at school. Glorious day

Jan. 15, Thurs. School. Made posters for <u>Hansel and Gretel</u> at school. Karl called and I showed him my Kodak book again. Shopped for new primers, etc.

Jan. 16, Fri. Marguerite's birthday. Karl and Fergie came to a dinner in the shack as a surprise for her. [The girls always knew when the cowboys had come to call by the jingling of their spurs as they dismounted.] Goodies from the Robinson's and cake from Mrs. Girdner. Candles and steak! Read aloud.

Jan. 17, Sat. Fried steak, and ironed for spring. Played in the dead leaves by the creek with Eva. The creek is "up," and as Marguerite says, looks like a chocolate soda.

Cornville, Arizona
January 18, 1914, Sunday

Dearest Mother,

   It seems appropriate on my birthday to give you something, so I am sending you a little check with which I hope you will buy a fountain pen. Alice and Aunt Mamie thought you would like one, and I send very much love. I am very glad I was born!

   I hope you will get this on my birthday. The creek is "up" from the melting of snow in the mountains, caused by a warm rain. It is high and swirling, and red brown instead of clear. Mr. Cox had an awfully exciting time crossing yesterday, and the mail couldn't go from here. It didn't get in on time today, and may not have come at all.

   I taught my class in Sunday school this morning, then had dinner and a rest and a walk and read Madeline Williard's book, <u>The King's Highway</u> M. had gone hunting all day with a school boy, so it was very quiet, with no callers, and only gossip from the doorway with a man on horseback in the road!

Do take care of Frisk. I'm sorry he is getting old. Is Hylinda doing any work now?

I expect to soon send a check to Alice to buy things for me, etc. and please take enough from that for the present for Janet [her cousin]. I may get some other little thing for her, too, since I used to be her special "crony"

I told you about the dinner I planned for M. It was lots of fun. Her birthday was Friday. We cleaned house after school, and a little before six P.M. I told her it was to happen. The "boys" arrived soon afterward (K. and F.), and helped prepare the meal. Mrs. Robinson (of Jerome) was a fairy godmother. She sent not only steak and a cake and nuts, but a big can of pineapple and two boxes of homemade candy. The steak was indeed a treat. Karl fried it, as we didn't have any way of broiling it. We had canned peas, and I made a salad put into scooped out apples, the potatoes were baked in Mrs. G's oven, as we have none. They were a luxury too, as she doesn't bake them. We began with Campbell's tomato soup, which is good. We had pineapple with the cake. Mrs. Girdner made the cake for M., all fussy, and there were candles for it I found left over from Christmas. Marguerite and Fergie "did dishes" afterward. M.'s box from home had some good things to eat. We surely appreciate a change in diet!

How I should love to be home on my birthday!

> My dear love to you and
> Papa, and all, Elsie
> P.S. Monday, mail expected
> today, tho creek still high.

Jan. 18, Sun. Read <u>The King's Highway</u> and finished <u>Quattrocentisteria</u>. Rested and walked by the creek.

Jan. 19, Mon. Told the story of King Arthur's birth, his swords and his marriage. Wrote some verses and wish I could do better! Read story of David.

Jan. 20, Tues. Wrote a birthday letter to Aunt Mamie. Began David Grayson's <u>Adventure in Contentment</u>.

Jan. 21, Wed. Told the story of David. Margaret asked awed, "Is that really a really?" Read in <u>Morte d'Arthur</u>. Karl and Fergie called. Karl played the mandolin.

Jan. 22, Thurs. MY BIRTHDAY. Beautiful letters from home. Two dinners, noon at Girdners', night at the shack with Karl and Fergie. Shaded candle. Gifts and thanksgiving.

Letter from Elsie's sister
Jan. 22, 1914

Sylvia Dearheart,

    This is just a little word for your birthday—which is so wonderfully different from the one a year ago! Whole cycles apart they are. You might have been the inhabitant of another planet a year ago so unsure you were of life's substantial gifts, because the flesh was weak but now you are here and a world of blessings will make this the richest new year of all. Not that its path is clear, but I believe it leads toward clearer light and deeper gladness.

    I am not going to write you any definite wishes. You know well enough that I wish you every lovely fulfillment, just as soon as God sees you are ready for the numberless gifts. I'm just thankful with you, beloved, and glad you are my friend for all the splendid years ahead; for the rich things your life will add with zest to mine. But my deepest wishes are written not on its pages but in your heart that will make no mistake in the deciphering.

                    God bless You Dear Elsie-Sylvia,
                    Your Ever Loving Alice

Cornville, Arizona
January 23, 1914

Dear Father and Mother,

    What delightful gifts you all sent me. We've had a regular feast, and have a lot of things left. Thank you very, very much. The things are all just what I wanted.

Before I say more about them, tho, I want to tell you how delighted I am over the thought of Mama's coming to Arizona. I'm glad you wrote me about it, Papa. Do persuade her to come. I'd just love to have her. Mama, if it would be good for you how would it be too extravagant? I don't believe you'll ever have a good long rest until you are somewhere where there isn't anything to do! You may never have such a good chance again. This would do you far more good than if the rest of the family were here, for you wouldn't have housekeeping to do here. Please come as my guest. For a while, at least, I'm sure Mrs. Girdner would take an extra boarder for dinners. I'd delight in having you as my guest. It might be a good idea for you to bring a small tent. A small trunk would hold that and your clothes. I'd love to have you stay until I go. School's out the 17th of April; only 12 more weeks more after this. If you got too tired of the monotony here, and missed Papa too much to stay that long, you could go home anytime, of course. They say February is always warm here.

You wouldn't mind the lack of "modern conveniences" and our crowded circumstances as much as some people. My only fear is that you would be very lonely. You'd like Mrs. G., tho, and we come home at noon, and usually soon after 4 P.M. nowadays. You could see me at recesses, and visit school when you liked. You could rest hours and read a lot and make things by hand for Alice's chest when you wanted to do anything like that. You'd like Mrs. Hurst and Mrs. Johnson, too, and could probably see them sometimes. I know you'd enjoy Eva and Stanley.

As Papa suggests, I might not send any money home if you were here, because I'd want to pay your fare both ways as well as have you as a guest. Please come! You don't know how glad I'd be to have you! Even our camp-Bohemian life I think wouldn't get seriously on your nerves. You'd rather like Karl and Fergie, who at times half seem to live with us.

The country here is lovely. I can hardly wait myself for the spring to come. It would be good for Alice to have more responsibility with you away, and I know Aunt Mamie would love to keep good care of Papa! I've been wishing so much you could all come, but had given up hope of that. You wouldn't have had a real rest that way, tho. The change of everything would probably make you fat. My, but I'd love to have you here with me! It would give me so much joy! You've never gone anywhere to visit any of your children, or anybody else when you were really away like this. You could just live out of doors. It is really lovely by the creek, even when the trees are bare.

If you came on a Saturday I could probably meet you. You would leave Los Angeles at about two on Friday afternoon, and be in the shack by bedtime on Saturday night.

I'll write more about it next time. You probably should telephone to the Santa Fe in Los Angeles to engage a berth, Papa. Please be sure to get one for her, tho it may cost a good deal. I think three dollars or so. Pay an extra 25 cents and you can keep the berth as far as Phoenix, instead of changing at Wickenburg. That's much better, as it is you'd have to change very early. By going down to Phoenix you don't have to get up until time to change cars at about 7 a.m. Then you go back in the new train over the same ground as far as Wickenburg. You get to Prescott about 1:28, but go on through with only a ten-minute stop. You can probably get your ticket in Long Beach for Clarkdale itself, from 20 to 22 dollars, I think. You'll need a lunch for Saturday, and probably would rather take your supper for Friday night, than to get off at. . . I forget the place where there's a Harvey House.[8] But please get your breakfast on the diner as soon as you get on the new train at Phoenix. It is such fun to think of entertaining you! I wish I could be with you on the trip. Be sure to get that breakfast, and get a good one. It will keep you from getting so tired on the journey.

Mrs. Girdner had a lovely cake for me, with the date, on the table. Eva gave me a handkerchief, and I got cards from them.

We had Karl and Fergie to supper, and had a grand meal, creamed tuna in toasted bread patties, large squares hollowed out; salad using the bananas and

---

8   Fred Harvey established restaurants at stops along the rail line for the Santa Fe railroad. He has been credited with civilizing the West. "Certainly he brought gastronomic delights and hospitality beyond many cattlemen's wildest dreams. He was known for high-quality food and service. In Arizona, Fred Harvey had the problem of getting fresh milk. Most of the herds there were not milk-producing herds. He established his own dairy farm in Arizona. Meals at the Harvey house were 75 cents until 1918 when they went up to $1. Harvey 'girls' (waitresses) were reported to have only lasted 6 months in the desert locations before they ended up marrying a rich mine owner or ranchman. The grand total of Harvey Girls who became Western wives has been estimated at 5,000. Fred Harvey demanded that gentlemen wear coats to the table." (Pamela Berkman, ed. *History of Atchison, Topeka & Santa Fe* [Greenwich, Conn.: Bromptom Books Corp., 1988]).

cherries I got; canned corn, and French fried potatoes. We had a fruit drink with the cherries in it; and in the center of the cake we put a large candle, shaded, with improvised shade & candlestick that were pretty with red paper. You should have heard what Karl and M. (and I!) said about the cake. The cake was very good. I thought I'd never tasted such good cake before. Then we had a pudding M.'s mother had sent her, and candy and Alice's delicious cookies. You were all so "lavish!" Papa, I expect to get your violets tonight, when we go to the office. I'll love to have them and the albacore, too.

PM: Two packages from you. I can't wait to open them. Drawers are fine, and bag lovely and just right size. Thank you for all, very, very much. Letter from Ernest tonight. Tell Alice and Aunt M. I like their things very much, and will write them next time.

I'll send you a check for $25 soon. Please tell A. I'd like her to send two or three rather late magazines the rest of you have read. I'd like a Harper's sometime. Don't try to send the ham. Hoping you will come, Mama.

With much love, Elsie

Jan. 23, Fri. Wrote to specially ask my mother to visit me. Played surgeon when Reymundo was hit in the head by a horseshoe. [It would have cost fifteen dollars to bring the doctor from Jerome. On another occasion Elsie treated Reymundo when he fell off his burro into cactus while trying to show off.] Rode to the post office. Read part of <u>Tristan and Iseult</u> to Marguerite.

Jan. 24, Sat. Tried to learn to play on M.'s mandolin. Rain and rain! Got our own dinner. Read R. Chamber's <u>The Gay Rebellion</u> to M., absurd book.

Jan. 25, Sun. Walked to the creek with Eva. Karl and Fergie came after supper, and Karl left without saying "goodnight!"

Jan. 26, Mon. School. Read afterwards. Night of wind, rain, and aches!

Jan. 27, Tues. Still rain. I have only two pupils in the morning and this day I am glad of it. Rested and decided to be sensible.

Jan. 28, Wed. A few more children. Cold winds. The snow on the Black Hills beautiful.

Jan. 29, Thurs. Cold last night, 11 degrees below freezing. Finished reading <u>The Little Lame Prince</u> to the 4th and 5th grades. Tried the mandolin again.

Jan. 30, Fri. Delightfully heavy mail and letters and books! Excited over home news. Will my little sister be married so soon?

Jan. 31, Sat. Lazy day. Marguerite and I dress for dinner, and the Girdner boys furnish a show by calling on us in disguise.

Feb. 1, Sun. After Sunday School—and I rest. I walk alone for dandelions. Fergie calls alone.

Feb. 2, Mon. Another day of glorious weather, with some school out-of-doors. Wrote letters in our dooryard.

Feb. 3, Tues. Finished <u>Adventures in Contentment</u>, and so loved the country more than ever. Began Moulton's edition of <u>Isaiah</u>.

Feb. 4, Wed. Made valentines at school. Missed Karl.

Feb. 5, Thurs. Thought of my sister Alice on her birthday. Walked by the creek after school. Read in <u>Joseph Vance</u>, entertaining.

Feb. 6, Fri. Read <u>Marie Claire</u> aloud to Marguerite.

Feb. 7, Sat. Went for a walk in the afternoon with Marguerite and at night with the children to the creek for water by moonlight. Finished <u>Marie Claire</u> aloud, wonderful book.

Feb. 8, Sun. Sunday school. School girls called, then came Fergie, and once more Karl. Fire by the creek, and moonlight, then Karl and I wrestled with fate for hours. Glasses broken.

Feb. 9, Mon. School. No joke after last night's breakage of glasses and results! Never the less, wrote another long letter, and read some <u>Ladies Home Journal</u> suggestions, "How May A Girl Know," which formerly I had shown Karl at his mother's.

Feb. 11, Wed. Walked alone to Sunday's scene and tried to think things out, but didn't! Karl came while we were at supper and announced his departure for the University. Moonlight and our haunt again, and good-bye (again!).

4

I Couldn't Make Promises

"It is odd the way men think they can't be just friends and have to have everything or nothing."

It had been over six months since Elsie took her teaching position in Cornville, and she was now recognizing that there were lessons and knowledge that couldn't be learned in books. These farmers and cattlemen seemed to her to be the very foundation of America. They lived so naturally, with their roots in the earth she loved. She saw in her schoolchildren that living a life dependent on the land had taught them industry, patience, and perseverance. These frontier families of Arizona were independent and resilient, both qualities Elsie valued.

If a life of comfort and ease in the city meant a severing of the bond with the earth that these farmers had, then which was the life for Elsie? She had felt this bond herself in California when she had lived summers on her father's apple ranch on the wild, beautiful Palomar Mountain. But she had returned each fall to the city and school. She had, as a young school girl, experienced the best of both worlds, and she felt a pull to each of these vastly different lifestyles.

Karl Hurst was certainly elegant compared to all the other cowboys Elsie had met. His mother's home was unlike the other small, rustic farmhouses along the creek. Elsie missed the gracious book-filled homes she had visited while attending college in Claremont. Mrs. Hurst's home had a piano, she knew how to set a "proper" table, and books seemed to be very evident, although Karl's own home was much more modest. Karl himself had an intensity about him that both excited and frightened Elsie. He was sure about his love for her, but he was just as sure that he could not confine her to the isolation of Oak Creek. Karl seemed to use no deception or mask with Elsie. He was like the land here—open and clear and clean. He had declared his love soon after they met and equally soon expressed his fear of her leaving. Karl loved his farm, but he longed for Elsie to love it with him. Perhaps when he sat beside Elsie on "her sycamore tree roots," he felt the excitement of new worlds and possibilities open up as she read to him.

Elsie was comfortable with this place that Karl loved. She would tramp through the hills in almost any weather and notice all the things he loved— the birds, the flowers, the trees. She could express what she felt for it so clearly. Maybe Karl felt Elsie's education allowed her to do this. Though education had not given the poetry to Elsie's soul, perhaps Karl thought that it allowed her to say what Karl himself only felt. She seemed to belong to both rustic and modern worlds. Could he expect her to stay in rural Arizona forever, and leave her former life completely behind? Elsie shared a warm friendship with Karl; she was sure she liked him, but he was not willing to settle for just friendship.

Karl perhaps felt that he needed to gamble everything to become someone Elsie would love. He would leave his beloved farm and creek and endeavor to become educated. It must have taken more courage to face going away and possible failure at school than facing the hardships and challenges of his rugged county life. Surely Karl feared failing. He must prove, if not to Elsie, to himself that he was worthy of her. Even though their age difference may not have troubled him, her education had created a barrier and obstacle that he must overcome.

That night beside the creek, when Karl told Elsie of his plans to leave soon for the university, she must have been overwhelmed. She wrote that they "wrestled with fate for hours." Elsie felt a keen sense of admiration for this tender, intense, and very direct young man. What if Karl graduated from university for her sake, but she still didn't feel she loved him enough to marry him? Elsie may have wanted to tell him to stay and that she loved him and accepted him as he was, but she could not. It seems a part of her wanted Karl to be educated. More than ever, Elsie was torn between these two worlds, and the thought of this unaffected, earth-loving man struggling in college stirred both her fear and admiration.

Feb. 12, 1914, Thurs. I still receive Valentines ahead of time, and love the children more than ever. Talk on Lincoln and patriotism. Walked with Ruth Hurst after school.

Feb. 13, Fri. Little Ruth Hurst was thrown and dragged by her pony last night after I left her. I sent her a note. Fun over Valentines. Inaugurated the Bird Club. Karl left Cornville [to enroll at the University of Arizona, Tucson].

Feb. 14, Sat. Valentine's Day. Helped M. get ready for the party for her room. I went twice to the creek for water. We toasted marshmallows there at the party

Feb. 15, Sun. Went to Sunday School, then helped put up a picnic luncheon and went with Fergie and Marguerite to Middle Verde with mule team to take back Karl's horse. Humorous situation! Lost in White Hills, out from 1 to 9 P.M.

Feb. 16, Mon. School again. Afterward read all of <u>The Spoilers</u> by Rex Beach before dinner. Rain falling.

Feb. 17, Tues. Dick Duncan came to school to warn children of creek, fast coming up. Cavalcade fled, horses and burros to beat the torrent. The schoolhouse emptied instantly, no "Teacher, may we?" Went to creek to get mud to drink! Set it aside in a bucket, most of it settles.

The children often rode burros to school.

Feb.18, Wed. Rain. Only 5 children at school. Went with Fern, Bessie and Eva at noon to see the creek decidedly "up!"

Feb. 19, Thurs. Still only five at school. Again went at noon to see the creek. I finished <u>Laddie</u> by Gene Stratton Porter. Like <u>Adventures in Contentment</u> it makes one want to marry a farmer!

Feb. 20, Fri. And again only five children! School out early. Creek still up, and still no chance for mail.

Feb. 21, Sat. Pancakes for breakfast-lunch, and cream toast for lunch-supper! Creek comes up higher, exciting, roaring brown torrent, logs flying by

Sunday February 22, 1914

Dear Family,

I'm afraid Papa's birthday gift and letter from me will be very late. The water was dirtier than ever last night. We played in the nice clean wet sand on the bank, like sea sand, only brown and a bit coarser. Then we were going to wash our hands, but decided it would be silly, as the water was thick with the same sand we had on our hands! I made fudge in the evening. When I poured water into the bowl to wash my hands after that it looked just like the fudge! We haven't been drinking much since, but today it is much better![9]

I haven't been able to send letters. Probably you thought of the creek. I do hope the creek will soon be crossed! Yesterday the creek was higher than ever, after a heavy shower. We heard it thundering, and all the Girdners and we hurried down to see it. It was grand! It was awfully rough and dark brown, and poured all through the trees, carrying great logs that flew by us. Today, tho, it is lower than for some time.

It is still cloudy, raining at intervals. I worked on Alice's towel yesterday, and enjoyed it. I fear I'm going to run out of the embroidery cotton. I enclose a sample, and would be much obliged for some more. It is absurd how very little I have sewn here. I feel like doing more now, and should love to make some things for Alice.

Some of the time today the sun has been out gloriously. The trees by the creek are budding, and alder tassels are out.

We got up late this morning. We made hotcakes out of pancake flour, using the larger of the little frying pans you sent, and raking coals to the front of the stove, as we do to make toast. It is fun. We had chocolate, too, made of milk because the water wasn't attractive! We had only two meals yesterday, got our own dinner, which was milk-toast, canned corn and pineapple chiefly! Also had chocolate malted milk.

I get so excited when I think of seeing you all! Won't we do a lot of talking, though! If I get a sudden chance to send this I may not have time to sign my name. I won't finish it now, as we may get the mail before we have a chance to send any.

Monday, Haste. This can be sent far as P.O.! Mail may come.

Much Love, Elsie

---

9   The irrigation ditch ran about fifteen feet from the Girdners' kitchen door and had an abundance of clear-flowing water except when there was a heavy rain in the Red Rock country twelve-to-fourteen miles up the creek. Then the water would be red.

Feb. 22, 1914, Sun. WASHINGTON'S BIRTHDAY No Sunday school due to creek. Sunshine! Read myths and in the Bible. Rested. Fergie came in the evening and stayed late. Fire and flashlights [homemade flash photographs].

Feb. 23, Mon. Still few children at school. Desperate for mail! M. and I walked as far as the Johnson's crossing but heard mail still absent. Got in quicksand. Slough!

Feb. 24, Tues. Glorious sun and an hour of school near the mesquites. Read a good deal in Le Morte d'Arthur.

Cornville, Arizona
Feb. 25, 1914

Dear Family:

Still no Mail! And I suppose you haven't had any from me for quite a while. I'm afraid none has left the P.O. yet. We really expect to get some today, 10 days since we've had any.

Papa, this is your birthday. I hope you are enjoying it very much and are having a sunny day. It is cloudy again here. The creek is down much lower now, almost normal, I imagine. I have 14 children today, more than for over a week.

The mail crosses the Verde River, into which Oak Creek enters. Our Oak Creek, they say, has sometimes been much higher, but the Verde never as high before as some days lately. Two or three men and several horses have been drowned in the Verde the last days in trying to cross. There is a bridge at Camp Verde, tho, 15 miles below here. Probably you will get this with my other letter. I don't seem to have much to say, except again about the creek! I'm very eager to hear from home.

Monday M. and I walked as far as the Johnson's crossing and learned no mail had yet come to the office. We followed the curves of the creek and found the wide slough harder than usual to cross. Several times one of us got one foot in above the shoe top, in quicksand. It was quite a trip!

My clothes are getting in great need of repairs and cleaning and replenishing, but I'll get along all right until school is out. I've been trying to wear almost altogether things that rarely if ever need laundering, especially since all our water is brought all the way from the creek by hand. I've been doing very little washing the last month.[10] By washing that Copenhagen blue dress and perhaps the heavy tan one, I'll get along beautifully.

The weather has been much warmer lately.

Fergie came to see us Sunday evening, and stayed late. We took some flashlights of our so-called "fire-place," made by opening the front of the stove.

I do hope you haven't been worrying because no letters have come. From now on the creek may come up again any time.

With much love to all, Elsie

Feb. 25, Wed. My Father's birthday. After school went to the most romantic spot on the creek! Jessie brot mail, dozen or so cards and letters from home and others, including Karl.

Feb. 27, Fri. Crisp and cross in school hours today, but received a nut and two apples and several gifts of flowers! Went to the creek and read the <u>Green Bough</u> and wrote letters and thought.

March 1, Sun. Glorious weather. After Sunday school went to the Johnsons' (eight on four horses!) for the day. Enjoyed Sunday afternoon at the P.O., visited with the Hursts there. Walked home after Doris "put us across" the creek. Fergie called.

A fun outing

---

10 When the water was muddy they carried water from the creek, set the tubs on rocks and built a fire. Lye was placed in the water, and it was boiled, causing the mud to foam up to be skimmed off.

March 2, Mon. Washington Day, sadly belated by the creek, and consequent lack of a decent sized school, now celebrated.

March 3, Tues. Began again having folk-dances for part of exercise. After school read <u>Joseph Vance</u> on Sycamore roots over creek.

March 4, Wed. Hours under (on and by) the Mesquites, even singing there. Read again on the roots. Buds swelling! <u>Joseph Vance</u> finished, good.

March 5, Thurs. Discussed bluebirds and colored pictures of them. Washed some clothes in the creek, and read by the creek. Ironed in the evening. Played tag with M.

March 6, Fri. Only 6 weeks left now! Told Bible story of Samuel. After school walked to post office, "put across" by the Johnson's. Windy and dusky before I got back.

March 7, Sat. Mr. Barron and F. Schuerman brot fish and a cake to luncheon. I went to schoolhouse and creek with Mr. Barron, and dug in Indian caves with him. Then rode with "the cowboy" Final meal by the creek. Fire and moonlight![11]

March 8, Sun. The Hursts called, and I "snapped" a picture of the dear tots. Then Fergie came, and we idled by the creek, and had a family party and supper and reading in the shack.

Cornville, Arizona
Sunday, March 8, 1914

Dearest Mama:

Friday after school I walked to the post office, "put across" the creek by the Johnson's. Your letter and card were there, with the embroidery cotton and sausage. Thank you very much for both. The sausage came just at an opportune moment, for we'd been wondering what we'd have to simulate a meat course for yesterday's luncheon. It is delicious and surely a change. M.

---

11 A Jerome newspaper account soon after this read, "Red Rock Notes: Fritz Schuerman and his shadow made a business call at Cornville on Saturday. We do not know what business was, but it must have been pressing, since they did not get home until midnight."

rejoices in it (as I do, too) and Mr. Baron asked me to tell you that one man surely appreciated it. He just raved when he saw it, and ate and ate! He said it was "like finding a gold piece where you haven't seen one for 15 years!"

He and the real cowboy, Fritz Schuerman of Red Rock, came about 12 yesterday, and didn't leave until about ten at night, despite the 15-mile ride ahead of them. The weather was glorious, F.S.'s sister sent a tiny frosted cake, and they brot fish they caught in the creek last night. We fried them and had the sausage, creamed canned string beans, a big salad, lemonade, biscuits made by Mrs. G., crackers, and then the cake, some floating island I made and "sea foam" made by M.

Afterward F. S. and I did the dishes. One of us was to ride to the P.O. with Mr. Schuerman on Mr. Barron's horse. M. flipped a coin to decide which of us, and she went. Then Mr. B. and I went to the schoolhouse and talked over schoolwork and later to the creek, then to some Indian caves. He's even wilder than I about these Indian things. We talked books until M. was disgusted beforehand. It was a pleasure to be again with someone who cared to talk of such things.

About six we ate some more, and then F.S. and I went for a ride. It was glorious! When we got back the four of us had a fire by the creek in the moonlight and ate yet some more! Coffee and crackers and wafers.

Three weeks from now they want us to come to Red Rock for a party, and stay over a night or two at Mrs. Loy's. We've met her husband, Mr. Loy, a cowboy. It would be great fun. Some of the cowboys would come for us with saddle horses. Some of the Jerome teachers we've met had a "grand time" staying there with these hospitable Red Rock people at the time of the dance we did not go to. They had wanted us to stay over if we had gone there. Mr. Barron raves about the friendliness and social life in Red Rock and thinks it's awful the people here aren't more sociable.

It is fairly hot to-day.

The Girdners wrote me a good recommendation to send with applications. They want me to be here next year. I wish I could be near home. I'd have to take exams just to teach in grammar school, I think. There are so many applicants for vacancies that I'm rather dubious about getting anything very good.

You ask when I could get home. So Alice really thinks of being married in April! We'll very likely engage someone to take us and trunks to Jerome or Clarkdale. We could probably leave here Sat. the 18th and I'd get home Sunday the 19th. I think the train is due in L.A. about ten in the morning. If we didn't get anyone to take us we'd have to leave here Sat. in order to get home before Thursday. Leaving here by stage, we'd have to stay overnight in Jerome, and unless we took the Sat. stage and so reach home Monday we'd have to wait here until Tuesday.

They say the creek's liable to come up at any time, due to the warm weather, or, of course, it might rain at anytime. So don't worry if you don't hear from me suddenly for a week or two, or even longer.[12] I don't expect this to happen. If it should get up near the time I'm to come home I may be able to go around by Camp Verde. I might not be able to let you know when to expect me. I might think it wiser to wait here a few days. So if anything like that should occur don't worry. In such a case I'd probably telegraph where to expect me, tho I might "surprise" you. Consequently, don't worry if you get a telegram. And above all don't worry because there's the chance of this trouble! I don't imagine there will be any such.

You asked about refreshments for the wedding. At Helen Hogle's wedding they had quite a feast, didn't they? At Mamie's, too, there were all sorts of things; I believe chicken patties and olives and a salad and coffee, etc., besides ice cream. But it would be foolish for us to try to do that when we can't rightly afford an expensive affair.

Tell Alice if she thinks of any particular things I can do I'll be only delighted to help. A bride isn't supposed to have to think of the decorating, for instance. I'd love to see to that with as many orders from her as she chose to give. Usually the bride's girlfriends covet the honor of helping with that, and maybe some boys!

Monday, March 9, 1914

Dinner interrupted my letter and then the Hursts called on us. The tots are darlings. I took a picture of them. I enjoy Mrs. H. Just after

---

12 *Williams News* article from March 12, 1914: "High waters of Oak Creek abated, 25 sacks of mail unloaded at Cornville due to rise of Verde River."

they left Fergie came and we ate candy by the creek. Later the three of us read or wrote letters at the shack until we had supper about nine. After that I read aloud until ten or after. The Girdner's had guests at dinner, so we saw a good deal of people.

Your letter came, and the package. I'm delighted to have the bread and will be careful about eating it. I hope you'll find something else as good for you. Do please take good care of yourself, Mother, dear.

Haven't time to answer your letter now. Wish you would feel you could have a new dress. I want you to use all that money, anyway. Just suit yourself.

Hope Alice went or is going to Elsinore with you. You and she must rest.

With much love, Elsie

Monday March 9, 1914

Dearest Papa and Mama,

I was very glad to have your letter, Papa. No, Mama, I hadn't forgotten your brown silk, but I think you ought to have a new one for the wedding. Still, I suppose you won't go "out" much at Elsinore! Please yourself, but I'd rather have you get a new one unless you really would feel better not to do it.

Don't try to send me anything else you make, Honey. Save your strength for all the many things to be done at home just now.

After school tomorrow we may go to call at the home of some of our children.

The peach trees are coming into bloom gloriously, and the mesa is green and some new wild flowers coming out. It looks like real spring. The buds on the cottonwoods are bursting, too. The place is very beautiful.

As the county superintendent is expected tomorrow I may not be well able to add to this then before Doris takes it to mail.

I do hope you are not working very hard now. You mustn't get all tired out! If Elsinore isn't too hot for my health I want to do a lot of housework this next summer, and give you a rest. I hope I can exist there! Also, I hope the rest of you can! When I remember how terribly sick I felt because of the heat there I surely hope it is cooler where the ranch is. [Her parents had decided to try living full-time at their ranch in Elsinore.]

> With very much love,
> Your loving daughter, Elsie
> P.S. Wed.—Co. Supt. seemed
> to like my work.

March 9, 1914 Mon. Folk dances lots of fun. Still thinking about Karl! Walked and enjoyed the spring.

March 10, Tues. Got ready for the County Superintendent.

March 11, Wed. Mr. Miller arrived and his visit was not as bad as I had feared.[13] Went home with Bessie Lee for a call, and brot home peach blossoms.

March 13, Fri. Began reading Alice in Wonderland aloud at school. Walked with Marguerite and Nellie to the first creek crossing to meet Jessie bringing the mail.

March 14, Sat. Worked on a lunch cloth for Alice. Wrote to Helen on my sycamore roots.

March 15, Sun. Went to Sunday school. Fried fish for supper. Then Fergie came.

Monday March 16, 1914

Dear Mama,

Yesterday I walked with Eva to the Bog and got maidenhair ferns. It is lovely there, up above a curve of the creek! We crossed the water on Nig. I

---

13 In her book *Ranch Schoolteacher* Eulalia Bourne, who was a teacher at the Beaver Creek School, eleven miles from Cornville, wrote, "Long ago county school superintendents could visit rural Arizona schools, at least distant ones, only once or twice a year. Usually they considered it good strategy never to let the teacher know when they were coming. If she thought the superintendent might drop in any day she kept herself and her lessons and schedules prepared for inspection at a moment's notice. A visit was a little like a spy method."

had been asked to go with M. Saturday. She made a call I wanted to make, too, but I had blistered my heel so a week ago that I didn't dare walk more.

Just after Eva and I got back, about dusk, Fergie came, and then soon M. and the girl, Jessie, to stay overnight. Fergie brot us apples and apple blossoms, and M. and J. some fish they had just caught. Fergie cleaned the fish and made the fire, and I made chocolate and scrambled eggs with sausage in them, and then fried the fish in butter in the chafing-dish. They were good! M. made lemonade and set the table, and the others helped in general. It was nine when we began eating. Then Jessie and I did the dishes while M. and F. went to the creek for water, and later Jessie and I toasted marshmallows while Fergie helped Marguerite with her 9th grade bookkeeping until after midnight! J. and I got so sleepy we didn't know what to do. In a house of one room one can't go to bed when a man is calling! Fergie and I certainly had a funny time. You see why I didn't get letters written yesterday! I did write one or two, to mama and to a girl who is sick.

I hate to keep asking you for things, but I need some! I'd like very much to have two rolls of Eastman Kodak films, 3 1/2 by 3 1/2 inches, six exposures in each film. Our last films have been used now. Will you please send 1 skein each of DMC 668, 3325, and 322, the kind like the sample enclosed? Thank you very much! I enclose a check for a dollar. There will be some left for other use later.[14] I don't know if Alice could get things for me very well now in Elsinore. I hope you don't miss the rest of the family too much. I hope somebody will persuade Hylinda to have a new dress for Alice's wedding!

With very much Love, Elsie

March 18, Wed. Disappointed in mail or lack of it! Embroidered on a lunch-cloth for Alice's chest. Washed a few clothes in the creek.

March 21, Sat. Washed and ironed, made out monthly school report, made cross-stitch pattern with Eva, applied at Williams, Arizona.

---

14 A dollar went a very long way. In 1911 a roll of six-exposure Kodak film cost only twenty cents (Eastman Kodak Co. brochure, Rochester, NY 1911).

March 22, Sun. Fergie came to drive us to the Hurst's. Beautiful day in all ways. Loved the "adorables" [Karl's two little sisters, Edna and Harriet] and played with them all day. Enjoyed Ruth and the rest. Saw Karl's house, walked to Pages Springs.

March 23, Mon. Art exhibition at school. Gave each child a choice of a Perry picture. [The *Perry* magazine promoted the use of inexpensive reproductions of fine art.] Their enthusiasm was delightful. Embroidered with Eva after the lesson.

March 24, Tues. Amused by Ruth's letter to "Buddy" [Karl Hurst] in fifth grade language. Enjoyed just talking to Geography class.

March 26, Thurs. Rode on a burro bareback and sideways at noon! Gathered dandelions by the creek after school. Talked to fifth grade about French Revolution.

March 27, Fri. Went to the Post office after school with Doris and Reymundo on Tot part way, then walking with Ruth. Waded the last curve on the way back. Wrote to Karl.

March 28, Sat. Expected to ride 15 miles to Red Rock, but owing to rain the cowboys and horses did not appear. Cut out house dress for Alice and worked on luncheon cloth.

March 29, Sun. Still raining now and then. Wrote many letters. Walked on hills with Eva and found flowers and saw rainbow. Fergie brot candy and mail and stayed fifteen minutes!

March 30, Mon. Showed the girls folk-dances after school. Sewed with Eva. Planned Arbor Day program with M. and got out of bed to write a small pageant for it!

March 31, Tues. Talked with the older girls again after school. Ruth said before Jessie and Myrlie that she wished "Buddy" would marry me, then I'd be her sister-in-law!!! Shouts. Embarrassment.

April 1, Wed. APRIL FOOL'S DAY Karl's birthday and seven weeks since I've seen him. Fooled a little! We were given chocolate-covered soap!

Cornville
April 2, 1914

Dearest Father and Mother,

Two letters from you, Mama, came yesterday, and one from Papa. I'm too busy to write much these days, but I'm certainly glad to hear.

Yesterday after school I washed and tonight I have some ironing to do. It is eight o'clock now!

Ruth Hurst is coming to stay all night tomorrow. She's quite excited over it. We are to have an Arbor Day program in the afternoon, and have been especially busy getting ready for it. I wrote a little set of verses to carry out one idea. The children are to represent the different kinds of trees that are common about here, each carrying a large branch of the proper kind, and saying two lines about it. All the branches are beautiful now, with their fresh new leaves. Apparently some of the children's families are coming tomorrow.

I'm writing applications to superintendents to ask if there are vacancies. I'd like to teach in Arizona again. I wish I could be nearer home!

We're teaching Eva embroidery, and she's making a little Easter gift for her mother, who doesn't know about it, much!

We were fooled in various ways yesterday, the first of April.

When there wasn't more than a mist in the air at most last night M. and I went for a ramble by the creek, just before dark, the water is very low now. I hardly think it will be high again this spring, to matter, at least.

Friday I went to the post office. Doris took me on her horse "Tot" (with Reymundo on also) at least half the way. Little R. got permission from his "madre" to walk the rest of the way with me by a trail I didn't know. Both he and Doris are very friendly with me, and devoted to each other. He entertained me very much, talking his baby-talk dialect, and teaching me some Mexican. By this trail only one crossing of the creek is necessary and that is the one nearest the Girdners'. After I left Reymundo near his home, coming back, I had to wade! It was cold, and in places near my knees, but fun, too. I was glad no one was near! My one regret was that my <u>Student Life</u> slipped, and floated, unread, downstream while I waded! The trail is very beautiful, at the foot of steep hills, and most of the way beside the water.

The wild flowers are lovely. The children bring them to school every day. Some are like Virginian field daisies; a number of the kinds are new to me. Aren't these alder tassels? I got them by the creek last night. There were Indian paintbrush, Mariposa lilies, Covina (sego) lilies, and fleabane daisies.

Please send this on to the rest of the family. As I accomplish more, my writing seems to get worse and worse!

I may walk to the office if the sky clears more. Unless it rains too hard I suppose Fergie will be here this evening.

Our little cottonwood tree by the shack is out in fresh leaves now. The trees by the creek are glorious.

Now I must stop and take a rest. I didn't get up until 10:30 this morning! I sat up until that hour last night working on the lunch cloth. The cross-stitch work is very easy to do with the canvas to help, and it's fascinating.

I think about Alice and you, particularly these days.

I hope Papa is enjoying ranch life, give him my special love.

> With very much love for you,
> Your loving daughter,
> Elsie

Monday, still raining. F. brot mail and candy yesterday, stopped only a few minutes. Eva and I went for a walk.

> Much love, Elsie

April 2, Thurs. Read more of Tennyson to fifth grade, by the stream and they loved it, especially <u>Oenone</u> and <u>Lady of Shallot</u>.

April 3, Fri. Arbor Day at school. Ruth stayed overnight.

April 4, Sat. After breakfast Marguerite and Ruth and Eva and I sewed. Then I went with Ruth as far as the mailbox. Helped Eva finish her gift for her mother. Moved our bed outside.

Cornville, Arizona
Sunday, April 5, 1914

Dearest People:

I've just come home from Sunday school. M. went today for a long walk to the top of House Mountain, but as it would mean a ten or twenty mile trip I decided it was too strenuous for me. She went with one, probably several, of the school girls.

Two weeks from to-day I'll probably be home! I wish I were going to see you all right away. I get so excited thinking about it! We still expect to get into Los Angeles Sunday morning. I hope someone will meet me there, at the Santa Fe Station.

The wind is blowing again today. It blew yesterday, but the night was glorious, and we took one bed out and both slept in it near our door. I surely enjoyed that. I want to sleep outside this summer.

Sometime ago I wrote to Aunt Mamie for the party favors I'm to give my children next Saturday. I hope they'll come in time. She sent, unasked, a bundle of Easter paper napkins that will be just the thing. Parties are more than a novelty to these children.

Friday I didn't get any letters from either Elsinore or Long Beach. May have double amount in today's mail. I hope we'll get it today and not have to wait for tomorrow. Last Sunday Fergie brot it (and some candy) to us in the afternoon, and stayed only a few minutes. He usually stays a few hours. Imagine he'll come in time for supper tonight. He has a standing invitation.

I did some scrubbing on our floor yesterday. The shack is a sight. It's so dirty and our clothes are getting so disreputable it's a good thing school will be out so soon! Eva brings wild flowers all the time. I hate to think of leaving this place, much as I want to come home.

Those weren't alder tassels I enclosed! I believe they were box-elder. Our Arbor Day program went off rather well, considering the informality, and the fact that we hadn't felt we could let the school give much time to it. Several parents (etc.!) were there. We had it at 1:00 o'clock Friday, and then school was out when it was over. I enjoyed having Ruth Hurst stay with us that night. Karl hasn't written to me for a long time. That may be another of his freak ideas, or the same reason why he wouldn't come often after a while, when he felt his suit was hopeless. It is odd the way men think they can't be just friends and have to have everything or nothing.

Now the water, heated on the chafing-dish, is ready to "do dishes." M. and I take turns. We rarely do them oftener than once a day, I swept etc. before S. S, and that with bathing and breakfast took all the time. We have water in the ditch now.

May you have a beautiful, Happy Easter
With very much love, Elsie

April 5, Sun. Sunday school. Fergie and I went alone to the creek, and there I was angry, and we both talked frankly afterward. Several kinds of heartache.

April 6, Mon. Finished reading <u>Hiawatha</u> aloud. Began Easter work at school. Try to get over depression. Do I wish mail days came oftener? Eight more school days. Began packing.

April 7, Tues. Ruth brot a note asking us to reconsider, so we went to the charivari after all. Glen walked to the Hursts' with us and we went with them. I held Harriet. Fergie brot us home. Like moving pictures, wagons trailing through moonlight. Noise and games.[15]

April 8, Wed. Sleepy. Rode to Post office on Nig. Mr. Chick said, "I'm sorry for you girls, you have to go back to California now, you've let George Moore escape you, and one or two others." Lovely ride home through the Spring.

April 9, Thurs. Hard day at school, children horrid, if they are dears. A caller too. Nellie Smith came to stay all night.

---

15 George Moore, a well-known bachelor cowboy, had just married. That evening the neighbors held a charivari, all gathering to play raucous music with various homemade musical instruments outside the home of the newlyweds. The rags they had stuffed in the chimney finally drove the honeymooners out. Once invited in, the "guests" played games and entertained the young couple.

April 10, Fri. Final making of Easter cards at school. In evening Eva helped prepare fishpond for the party. Jessie brot piles of letters from Williams, Ariz., Kenneth, and Karl at last.

April 11, Sat. Thirty children coloring eggs in the shack! Good thing beds were outside. Then games by the creek. Rodeo meeting held in the schoolhouse and Eugene Barron brot two cowboys to a supper by the creek. Great Day!

Cornville, Ariz.
Sunday, April 12. Easter

Dearest People:

Easter greetings! I've had a lovely day, and hope you have. There were 34 at Sunday school and I enjoyed talking with my class about Easter.

Party for youngsters went off well, and we all had one grand time, tell you about it when I see you. Everything came in time but paper plates, and as we finally served things, thirty infants on the floor (beds outside) we didn't need them at all. All things were fine, and I'm much obliged. We had games by the creek.

The Round-up (Rodeo) meeting was held at our schoolhouse yesterday. Oh the cowboys riding by! Mr. Barron came, too, and brought two of them to supper with us by the creek, very interesting. The 5 of us cooked (he stayed overnight at schoolhouse and took one of our beds up) and Mrs. G. asked him and us to breakfast. Then he went with us to Sunday school. Fergie came in the afternoon.

We four went to a lovely "gulch" we've wanted to see. M. and I riding and the men walking beside us (except over creek!).

It's late now, and they've just gone. Enjoyed it all.

Last week was busy and this one may be worse.

I have a chance at a school in Williams, Ariz. High school work. If they telegraph it will be worthwhile for me to apply in person. I'll stop over there (only an hour or so ride from Ash Fork), and so go home by Ash Fork instead of southern route. It will be Santa Fe anyway. I'm sorry I can't know now. May not hear from them and then will come via Phoenix and get into Los Angeles Sunday A.M. about 10. You can phone to see just when train is due. If they send me a wire I might not get it until Friday night, so might not be able to tell you by letter. Probably I'll send a telegram to you to Long Beach, from Clarkdale Sat. A.M., telling you whether I'll get in Sunday or not. If I go to Williams, I'll probably stay overnight, leave there Sunday, near noon, and get home Monday about 8 A.M. I can make connections with main line at Cedar Glade, and take train going either north to Ash Fork or south via Prescott and Wickenburg (near Phoenix) and Santa Fe timetable will enlighten you.

Hate to say good-bye here, but I'll surely be glad to be home. I can hardly wait now, yet can't realize how soon it will be.

It seems queer I won't see Karl again before I leave Arizona. He writes that he mustn't think of anything, or say it, because he has two more years! I couldn't make promises anyway; and I'm glad he's there. Hope to see Mrs. Hurst and "the babies" to say good-bye.

If I go to Williams should get there about 4:30 P.M. Sat. Know of good hotel at the station. Don't worry! I'm twenty-six!

Much love to you everyone. Tell A. I fear I can't begin cap or finish dress, but can do that after I get home now. Glad to hear the date.

> Love again, and see you soon, D. V.
> [*Deo Volente*, Latin for "God willing."]
> Elsie

April 12, Sun. EASTER. Mr. Barron, having slept at the schoolhouse, was invited to breakfast by Mrs. Girdner, and so were Marguerite and I. Then he and I went to phone, lunch and to Sheep Head's Gulch with Fergie. Supper in the shack for four. Last Sunday

April 13, Mon. Sleepy! Rush of work to be finished at school. Only three more days of teaching on Oak Creek! Packed and sorted after school. Serene.

April 14, Tues. 11:40 P.M. Children helped me look over textbooks at school. Went home with Ruth, stayed to supper and was brot back by Fergie horseback. Hated to say good-by to the Hursts.

April 15, Wed. Ruth Hurst came and stayed overnight. Packed in the evening.

April 16, Thurs. Last day of school. Ruth for breakfast. Told <u>Lady of the Fountain</u> by the ditch. Almost wept parting with the children. Girls helped put away books. Mable stayed overnight.

April 17, Fri. Last day on Oak Creek. Mable, Jessie, Eva, Myrlie, Elon, and Nellie helped pack. It is twenty minutes before two A.M. (Sat.) and Fergie still here. Last fire!

April 18, Sat. Left Oak Creek 7:15. Left Clarkdale 11:10. Said Goodnight to Marguerite at Cedar Glade. At night met the school board at Williams. Stayed at Fray Marcos Hotel.

April 19, Sun. Waked by trains and phone in my room. Civilization a shock after the wilds. Left Williams about noon after visit with Mrs. Miller of the Board. Beautiful Scenery

8 o'clock dreary moon.
Timid lover coming soon.

By the doorway maiden waits.
How her heart palpitates.

Timid Lover's plans matured.
Moonlight kindly keeps obscured.
While the sun shines so gay
homogenus makes the hay, but—

Anxious Margie thinks of dew.
From the doorway sees tableaux.

April 18, '14
Lover gone—maiden flown—empty
shack sits all alone.
Moral- "Faint heart never won fair lady."

Mrs. Girdner, playing the matchmaker, drew these illustrations and mailed them to Karl the day Elsie left Cornville.

5

Resolves Aren't Easy to Keep

"Decided not to think so much about someone on Oak Creek."

As Elsie packed to leave Cornville I am sure she reminisced about all the fun she'd had teaching these exuberant children. The older children had been full of mischief and pranks. Once, Glen Girdner and his friends had filled a couple of old whiskey bottles with tea and proceeded to pretend they were drunk. This episode had briefly shocked and horrified Elsie and Marguerite, particularly as they offered the astounded teachers a drink of "whi'kkey." Parting with her much-loved children would be difficult for Elsie. She would also miss the adventures and the beauty of Cornville, although perhaps not the isolation. Her one year had been so full of memorable experiences. Now, however, teaching in Williams would be a chance for Elsie to fulfill her dream of instilling in older children her love of literature.

Elsie would be making the most of her trip to California by visiting all the places that held a place in her heart. Long Beach was quite a modern city, and it was there that Alice's wedding plans would occupy Elsie for the next month. Long Beach was also a contrast to their small family ranch in the isolated village of Elsinore. Long Beach had the cool ocean breezes, whereas Elsinore, since it was 40 miles inland, had a dry, desert climate. Pomona College, where she would reconnect with friends, was in Claremont, 45 miles north-east of Long Beach, and was located near the lovely San Gabriel Mountains.

There would be a stark contrast in the people to whom Elsie would be returning. Her family now lived a quiet, country life in Elsinore. However, when she returned to Pomona College to visit, Elsie's friends were attending plays and weekend house parties. The people and places she would visit in California would be nothing like the previous eight months in Arizona.

LONG BEACH, CALIFORNIA

April 20, 1914. Mon. HOME! On the train waked with joy and dressed at 5:30 to see Claremont and Mt. Baldy Los Angeles at 7:10 A.M. No city life for me! Home and Mother at 10 A.M. Excitement. Relatives came for dinner.

April 21, Tues. Talked and talked and talked. Unpacked my trunk. Ernest and Alice showed more of their preparations, and Ernest sang.

The "Triumverate" 1907 - Ruth Stailey, Caroline Harnett and Elsie. Caroline died in 1907 in a kitchen fire; by 1914 Ruth was seriously ill with TB. These best friends interwove their initials and their hearts.

April 22, Wed. Wrote business letters. Applied at Albuquerque. Went downtown and to the Pike.[16] Ernest seems to belong.

April 23, Thurs. Would apply at Nogales if it were not for the War [Nogales was a border town].[17] Cooked two meals, washed dishes, and gathered fresh roses, sewed on house dress for Alice.

April 25, Sat. Housework of various kinds. Helen came and I rejoiced. We talked about men, etc. etc. until 2 A.M. Good to talk of things worthwhile.

---

16 The Pike became a world famous Long Beach, California amusement zone in 1902 along the shoreline south of Ocean Boulevard. It had independent arcades, food stands, gift shops, a variety of rides and a grand bath house. *The Pike*, http://en.wikipedia.org/wiki/The_Pike

17 On April 9, 1914, in Mexico General Huerta briefly seized Americans in Tampico, Mexico, and President Wilson mobilized fifty-two war ships. On April 23 Mexico condemned the U.S. seizure of the Mexican seaport of Veracruz and ordered the US out of Mexico. (*Chronicle of the 20th Century*).

April 27, Mon. Wrote business letters. Shopped, bought blue coat, dress material, blue poplin, etc.

April 28, Tues. Dressmaker here, helped sew and cleaned my Panama hat.

April 29, Wed. Day in Los Angeles. Called on Ruth. Good to see her again, tried not to worry about her.

April 30, Thurs. Dressmaker here again. I helped with Alice's sewing and my own and did some housework. Walked with Alice and Ernest.

May 1, Fri. Rainy May Day. Sewed, sewed, sewed. Cooked and washed dishes, and walked after supper with Mama and Alice. Strenuous living!

May 2, Sat. Housework and sewing and shampooing. Spent the evening addressing wedding invitations.

May 4, Mon. Sewing and housework. Helen came for overnight and I enjoyed her. Encouraging letter from Karl!

May 5, Tues. Sewing and shopping. Bought bridesmaid gown and began it. Worked on a dress for Alice.

May 6, Wed. Still sewing and shopping! Packed my suitcase for Claremont the Beautiful.

CLAREMONT, POMONA COLLEGE

May 7, Thurs. Claremont. Met by Mrs. Darling, back with Kenneth! Mt. Baldy grander than ever. Such joy!

May 8, Fri. Dr. Parker's philosophy class with Kenneth. Senior chapel, auto ride with Mrs. Maynard. Call on Mrs. Humphrey May Dances with the Stoughtons.

May 9, Sat. Went with Kenneth Darling to L.A. to hear marvelous Flonzaley Quartet, rest for the soul. With him at night, Greek theater to see <u>Arizona</u>!

May 10, Sun. At the Roof's in Claremont! Visit with Mrs. Darling and church with Kenneth. Service strengthened my belief in Idealism.

Elsie dancing with Thornton Wilder, a college student at Berkeley, not yet a famous author.

LONG BEACH

May 11, Mon. Home again. Interesting good-bye to Mrs. Darling and Mrs. Stoughton.

May 13, Wed. Made Boudoir cap for Alice, sewed on other things.

May 18, Mon. Superintended a thousand things. Decorated. Alice's friends working. Guests arrived and Papa and Aunt Mamie.

May 19, Tues. Alice's wedding! Ernest became my brother. All was beautiful and the out-of-door space lovely. I was glad to be maid of honor. Went after by auto. Tried not to shed tears.

May 20, Wed. Helped Papa and Hylinda get ready for Elsinore, and saw them off. Straightened house with Aunt Mamie. Rested and went to bed early. Missed the absent ones.

May 22, Fri. Alice and Ernest came back from their wedding trip to Catalina, and were received with rejoicing.

May 23, Sat. Memories of Triumvirate. Marguerite spent the day with me. We went together to my first movie for some ten months, and talked Arizona!

May 24, Sun. Went to church with Mama and Aunt Mamie. Went out to Harnetts' as of old, and had tea there. Talked of Ruthie.

May 25, Mon. Shopped for next year at Williams! Fred came to supper and Alice and Ernest were the chaperons! Played Five Hundred.

May 31, Sun. Alhambra. Went to Baptist Sunday school where Fan plays in Orchestra.

June 6, Sat. Apartment Life Theater, <u>Peg O' My Heart</u>, wholesome, and refreshing and sweet.

June 8, Mon. Came out to Ruth's for my visit here. She is better! Talked and talked of two men!

June 9, Tues. On a couch in the sun in grassy back yard with Ruth.

June 10, Wed. Went downtown with Ruth and Earl, then to Long Beach to the Harnetts'. Walked with Ivy to Signal Hill, as of old.

Pomona College Girls - Elsie second from left

June 12, Fri. Shopped in the city on my way to Pasadena. Had a beautiful visit with Mamie. Talked until 12:00 of Alice and Lois and someone else.

CLAREMONT, POMONA COLLEGE

June 13, Sat. Claremont. Came to this blessed place, to the Maynard's. Called on Mrs. Darling and talked with Mary Beck, who is to teach in Cornville this year; tried to give her incentive to help my children. Class supper with Kenneth Darling, Elijah at Greek theater.

June 16, Tues. Class meeting, chapel program, class luncheon with Ethel Stailey Mrs. Darling at the Inn. Dinner with Kenneth and then Jimmy's splendid play in Greek theater.

June 17, Wed. Commencement Day Academic procession and commencement. Kenneth's violin solo and his "Summa." Helped decorate the Inn for banquet. Reception and banquet with Deak.

June 18, Thurs. Went with Deak to the Darlings. Luncheon at the Humphreys'. Farewell to the Darlings, saw them off for Europe and felt it.

ELSINORE

June 19, Fri. Wrote letters on the train. Garage man brought me out to the ranch. "HOME?" Yes! Glad to be with my family

June 22, Mon. Settling. Finished living room curtains. Painted most of Hylinda's floor. Hard work, but interesting. Making the place a home, all helping.

June 26, Fri. HOT ! 106 degrees in Elsinore. Worked a little out of doors and settling.

July 2, Thurs. Rose very late to have a good rest. Made soldier cap favors for the Fourth; read later than I should. Decided not to think so much about someone on Oak Creek.

July 3, Fri. Preparations for the Fourth, chiefly candy making. Resolves aren't easy to keep.

July 5, Sun. Family breakfast and "family prayers," all seven of us. Quiet day for Aunt Mamie and me together alone. Browsed in Emma, Wordsworth and the Bible. Walked.

July 6, Mon. Mama and I made a crepe dress for me, and began another. Talked with Hylinda. Asked for light.

July 8, Wed. Sewed. Pat came out for me in the machine, and I went for overnight with her. Movies and "The Arbor" and the lake.

July 11, Sat. Sewed, doing some finishing on dresses, and beginning blue slip. Cleaned my Panama hat. Some housework between. Too much with hands?

July 13, Mon. Cooked and ironed and studied. Clothes really getting in order. Hate to have to spend so much time on them, even in preparation for a year.

July 14, Tues. Sewed and cooked and drove chickens. Had a nap. Interesting letter from Karl Hurst.

July 15, Wed. Canned peaches, cooked (including baking of a cake), rested, wrote letters, ironed. Do this life or not?

July 16, Thurs. Canned and cooked, and studied history, and drove downtown. Letter from my Ruth, God Bless her!

July 26, Sun. A quiet Sunday at home. Read in the prayer book, imagining church at Williams.

July 28, Tues. General housework. Fresh spiritual calm.

July 31, Fri. Six weeks ago to-day I came to Elsinore. Four weeks from today I should be in Williams. Alice next week! Later. . .? Perhaps!

Aug. 1, Sat. Why don't I take more interest in society? Pat told me today of her house party to come, but I felt too disappointed over the loss of a quiet visit with Helen to take much interest in it. Read war news.[18]

SAN DIEGO

Aug. 4, Tues. To Oceanside by auto, then train to San Diego. Afternoon with Alice in her room. Mr. Gilmore took us to Susan's.[19] Went with her and her mother to Spreckles Theater, Inner Shrine. Much of gladness.

---

18 "Germany had just declared war on Russia, first shots fired" (*Chronicle of the 20th Century*).

19 Myron T. Gilmore was the wealthy president of San Diego Trust and Savings Bank. He was Alice Parker's uncle and had raised her. Susan was Alice's cousin.

Aug. 5, Wed. Spent the day with Alice, with luncheon in her beautiful home. Rested! Went with her and Susan to Exposition grounds, and at night with Susan and her mother to "movie."

Aug. 6, Thurs. Visited classes with Susan at Normal Summer School, and saw Mission Cliff Gardens and Palomar! Irene Jamieson at lunch. Three of us with Alice to Coronado Island for supper and concert. Wanted more than I can have.

LOS ANGELES

Aug. 7, Fri. Los Angeles, Alice helped in re-birth of aspirations. Rested a half hour in her room. Stayed over with my Ruth in Los Angeles. Had a good talk with her all evening on the porch.

Aug. 8, Sat. Still with Ruthie. Slept late and talked and rested all day, made candy for her. Try to be serene for her, and full of hope.

LONG BEACH

Aug. 10, Mon. Long Beach. Long farewell to Ruthie, then shopping and a little visit with Marguerite at a movie. Supper at Ivy Cottage, visiting Alice and Ernest.

BALBOA

Aug. 13, Thurs. Balboa, Special delivery letter from Helen brought me here. Mr. Montgomery Douglas also here for the evening. I like him enough!

Aug. 14, Fri. Quiet day of readjustment of friendship, ending in joy. On the sands by the surf, then rowing on the lagoons, just with Helen.

LONG BEACH

Aug. 15, Sat. Long Beach. Enjoyed a peaceful morning, and then regretfully fled the house party, and returned here.

Aug. 17, Mon. Studied geography and enjoyed being with Alice. Went to the Harnetts' for overnight. Aches and joys there.

ELSINORE

Aug. 20, Thurs. Wrote letters, and began packing in the trunk Aunt Mamie gave me. Walked in twilight with Aunt Mamie and Mama.

Aug. 25, Tues. Sewed on black and white serge Mama is making for me. Lovely drive about lake in machine with the family. Letter from Karl that

. . .

Aug. 27, Thurs. Packed etc. Hate to think this is last day with my family for so long.

Aug. 28, Fri. Train left Elsinore at 1:12; hating to say good-bye to my family. Pat helped them to see me off. Read and wrote on the train, going to bed in a berth.

WILLIAMS, ARIZONA

Aug. 29, Sat. Breakfast on diner, at 7:25 reached here, met by Mr. Winans, Mr. Youngblood and Minna Wissing. Breakfast again at the Winans' then got settled in new home, "The Dovecote," with glee. Mr. Y. helped us "lay in groceries." Reception for teachers at night.

Aug. 30, Sun. Went to Episcopal Church with Miss Collins, and liked it. After dinner went 30 miles with the Polsons in their machine to their

Williams Train station, the Fray Marcos Hotel and Harvey House Restaurant.

cattle ranch, the "Flying H." Wrote home. Mr. Youngblood and Mr. Gold called. Feel much at home.

Williams, Ariz.
Sunday, Aug 30, 1914

Dearest Family:

It doesn't seem as if it could be only yesterday I arrived and feel so much at home! So little time! People are outdoing themselves trying to welcome us. This morning Miss Collins, a teacher, called for me to take me to the Episcopal Church, as Minna Wissing and Georgia Alcorn, the girls of the house, were going to the Methodist Church. I enjoyed it very much. The rector, or whatever they call him, is very young, but gave a sermon exceedingly worth hearing, and of course I enjoyed the service. I had told Mr. Winans I was sorry not to be going to his church. He is a dear sort of father to us, lives very near. Mrs. W. is in Los Angeles just now. Then there's her mother, whom we call "grandma" immediately. I like them very much.

This afternoon (after a good dinner we got in a few minutes, of canned beans, warmed-over canned peas creamed, cheese, tomato and lettuce salad, and cantaloupe) we went for a wonderful drive. Mrs. Polson, a splendid woman (with children in school and a son 20 to 30) who lives near, asked us to go in their big beautiful new auto, her husband driving. We went to his cattle ranch, the Flying H (Brand H, you see), a 30-mile trip. The scenery is grand. For miles we went through the pine covered hills and meadows bright green and flecked with gay flowers, then through grassy valleys and cedar slopes. It was wonderful! We passed 2 or 3 ranches, the only dwellings, and some cowboys. The country, at this altitude reminded me of Doane and Mendenhall Valley on Palomar. We went about 1000 ft. lower than Williams which is, I think, 6700 feet high, population 1500. It is 8 o'clock now, and I must go to bed. The altitude is such a tonic I feel refreshed despite the full days. Tomorrow we will do very little work, may not stay at school half a day.

We enjoyed the reception last night, good speeches, good music, with lots of ice cream and cake, and a good chance to meet school people. It was rather exclusive.

Apparently, it is very hard for teachers to find satisfactory rooming and boarding places here, and I think I'm really very fortunate. This wide pretty house of 5 rooms, one all to myself, gives me chances to rest and have independence I might not get as a roomer. It is homelike and very pleasant, too. I like the girls, Minna is from Indiana and Georgia from Tennessee, both seeing the West for the first time. They got here Friday. Isn't it odd, where I'm Western?

The Williams people of the better class seem to be unusually fine ones. We went to dinner at the place where I would have so expensively boarded, with Mr. Youngblood Sat. The people there we liked much, the Golds. All these people are so hospitable I feel as if I'd known them always. Mr. Gold is an eminent citizen and spoke last night. He has such dry humor in joking with us! We seem to have callers any hour. He stopped in today because he was with Mr. Youngblood, the Superintendent. Mr. Y. has known Minna for years in Indiana. Though I've heard a rumor that he is engaged to another teacher here, he comes all the time to our house! Mr. Winans suggested we call it the Doves Nest. Mr. Gold at another time suggested "Seldom Inn"!

The town swarms with little children! The streets are all dirt and the sidewalks wooden. The citizens say it is a very safe place so long as one doesn't wander at night into the saloon section, which I think is farthest possible from us.

We rent our house from another very fine citizen who spoke last night, Mr. Curatin, formerly Supt. here. He lives on a ranch near and offers us beans if we'll walk over for them.

Yesterday we got remarkably settled as the house had been cleaned. The place looks very cozy. I'll send a diagram later.

It has showered a little and is almost cold a good part of the time! The sunsets both nights have been marvelous! These pine covered hills all about the town are most beautiful. Hope it is cooler with you.

Mr. Youngblood saw to trunks and countless other things for us. He must be near 30, but acts like a kid, and we can't help being so unceremonious with him that I don't know what we'll do at school! We can probably be dignified there! He took us over to the schoolhouse (practically only across the street) yesterday. My room is light and airy and new with glorious views of Bill Williams Mountain from my desk itself. The school is very well equipped, for example, has that 20 volume <u>Book of Knowledge Children's Encyclopedia</u>! He went to town with us, too (only a few blocks), and helped us shop. We had a huge list of groceries, etc.

It must be almost 8:30 now and I really am going to get into bed. I'm in my bathrobe on the bed (a double bed) now.

I do appreciate all you all did to help me off. I love you very, very much. I think school arrangements, etc. will be easy for me. We can have almost an hour at home at noon, for instance.

With very much love, Elsie

August 31, Mon. School opened by assembly, band playing splendidly. Met my children and liked them. Proud of the school. Worked on textbooks in afternoon. Mr. Youngblood like one of the family!

Sept. 1, Tues. First regular day of school. Keen joy for me, trying to give the children inkling of what year could mean, talking over work, etc. Heard Edna might come, and walked to glorious hillside.

Sept. 2, Wed. Met Helen's train at 7:25 A.M. and before 8:10 A.M. showed her school. Seems as if I had been here four months more than four days.

Williams School 1914

Sept. 3, Thurs. Busy day at school. We all wrote "poems" with chorus of "altitude" in evening! Mr. Youngblood went with us at 10:15 P.M. to meet Helen. Good night visit with her.

Sept. 4, Fri. From 6 to 7:30 Mr. Youngblood, Minna, Helen, and I tramped on the beautiful ridge. Said good-bye to Helen and received a telegram from Karl. Met him dizzily at 6:30 after 7 months separation. He came to dinner. From 10 to 12 we walked by lake through pines. I am proud of him!

6

New Epoch in My Life

"*Hard good-bye at night. I realize this begins new epoch in my life.*"

Karl's surprise visit seems to have changed their relationship into "friendship." But even the interest of a new life in Williams could not replace her persistent memories of him. As Elsie adjusted to life without him, she also faced the possible loss of Ruth, her dearest friend. In the months ahead the necessity for courage increased.

Sept. 5, Sat., 1914. Beginning a new epoch. Karl and I rested on the ridge until middle afternoon. Hard readjustments. Silent lunch for two, then in the evening he and Mr. Youngblood and Mr. Polson, the girls, and I went to the movies and later had a party of our own. Still more proud of him despite. . .

Sept. 6, Sun. Karl and I read the paper together, and then went to church. Odd to have him carrying my prayer book! He took us all to dinner at the Fray Marcos Hotel and me to Frontier Day. Hard good-bye at night.

Sept. 7, Mon. I realize this begins a new epoch in my life. Say "courage" to myself. Met Edna for her hour between trains, and with her saw Karl only for greeting, not even introduction.

Sept. 9, Wed. Try to get control of my new boy at school, who is hard to manage.[20] Everything seems queer these days.

Sept.10, Thurs. School, still feel queer! Mrs. Curatin and her children called, also Mr. Youngblood (here for dinner) and Mr. Gold. Hospitable Williams!

Sept. 11, Fri. Gave a geography examination. Getting used to my new room at school. Washed some clothes, dinner with Mr. Y. at the Gold's! Georgia and I walked.

Sept. 12, Sat. Remember it is Eva's birthday. Thought of Oak Creek and wrote to Marguerite. I have been here two weeks. Shopped.

Sept. 13, Sun. Letter from Alice Marie Parker before I was up gave new life and thankfulness. Georgia went to church with me. Dew Drop Inn dined at the Fray Marcos. Rested, walked with the girls, and went early to bed.

---

20 The school board felt that Elsie needed a year to prove she could handle discipline problems of sixth and seventh grade before she attempted to teach literature to high school students.

Sept. 14, Mon. Cook week for me began. Enjoyed first day of it immensely

Sept. 16, Wed. Enjoyed school, also cooking. Downtown (but no mail!) after dinner. We three and Mr. Y. began Spanish lessons under High School youth, Lilo Padilla, fun!

Sept. 17, Thurs. School does have worthwhile opportunities, yet had a visitor rather hard to appreciate. [A school trustee?] Mr. Y. stayed to dinner, and went down town with us, and spent evening.

Sept. 18, Fri. Cheered by finding my school visitor of yesterday apparently appreciated me better than I did her! Enjoyed shopping and cooking. Spelling match at school. Good visit with Minna at night.

Sept. 19, Sat. Climbed "Bill Williams" mountain, 14 mile trip, horseback, and climbing afoot on the peaks. Pines, aspens, peaks, view of "Mingus."

The US Forest Service fire lookout on the 9256 ft. summit of Bill Williams Mountain, c. 1910. Photo USFS

Elsie and teachers with Forest Service guide. Teachers all wearing Middy blouses, exercise wear of the time period.

Mr. Y., Minna, Miss Reese, Miss Peet, Miss Watson and I. A letter of strength and uplift from Alice M. Parker as I left. A day of glory, near to God, stronger for man. At night a letter from Karl that meant pain. I wrote him then.

Sept. 20, Sun. A strange day. Thought it wise to read the <u>Saturday Evening Post</u> in bed, instead of going to church. "The family" (including Mr. Y.) went to the Curetons' for dinner. Wrote letters in evening.

Sept. 21, Mon. Interesting new boy at school, Willard, aged 19. Full and busy school day. At 4:10 listened to band, then corrected papers and bought pottery from Indians on street. Rode horseback and helped buy a "family" horse. Played basketball in the evening.[21]

Sept. 22, Tues. Housecleaning and washing besides school. In the evening a mock trial at Mr. Gold's, Miss Reese the defendant, and we the witnesses!

Sept. 23, Wed. Prepared for exams at school. After school walked alone on the hills, and nearly slept under a pine. Read Wordsworth and found nature a blessing. Spanish class.

Sept. 25, Fri. My children brought me gifts. Georgia and I had a splendid climb by the dam. Mr. Y. here for supper.

---

21 Pomona College had a girls' basketball team in 1912 and 1913. Prior to that the Pomona College annual *Metate* lists only tennis as an option for women's sports.

Sept. 26, Sat. Corrected papers and cleaned house and bought a red outing hat! Went to my first card party and wondered if it is worth while? Fine people in Williams.

Sept. 27, Sun. Rainy out-of-doors day. We went on our horse to Coleman Lake, a 20 mile trip through pine forests and rain. Dinner under a pine tree with first rain.

Sept. 28, Mon. School and extra work on examination papers and reports. After basketball (where I enjoyed both the game and my children) worked until 1:20 A.M. Still rain.

Sept. 30, Wed. Rode through the woods beyond the lake, "Canyon Road." Mr. Miller, Supt. of lumber mill, and his wife went with us through the mill. Very interesting. Aches today.

Oct. 1, Thurs. New incentive at school for new month. Judge Layton, Co. Supt., visited school. Meeting of Women's Club after school. Spanish class in evening. Too busy.

Oct. 3, Sat. Rain kept us from the trip planned to Three Hills, but had a pleasant quiet day at home. Washed a little and shopped.

Oct. 4, Sun. Taught ten tots, aged 4 and 5, in Methodist Sunday School, and then went to St. John's to church. Rode a little (after awful attempt at Chinese Restaurant!),[22] and we three enjoyed the hill.

Oct. 6, Tues. After school cooked. In evening read <u>The Girl with the Green Eyes</u>, exciting play by Clyde Fitch, and <u>The Servant in the House</u>, inspiring play.

Oct. 8, Thurs. Received letter that made me feel happier. After school went to Literary Section of Women's Club, interesting. Georgia and I went to the "movies" with Pete Campbell.

Oct. 9, Fri. School is interesting and with wonderful opportunities. I coached my little girls in basketball. Mr. Y. and we three had a picnic supper on the hill above the lake, venison, tomatoes, bread and coffee!

---

22 The historical marker database for Williams, Arizona, describes the Telzlaff building (designed as a saloon and bordello built in 1897 by German tailor August Telzlaff) as having a Chinese restaurant with an opium den at the back of the building.

Oct. 10, Sat. Marketing and cooking and callers in morning. Trimmed my inexpensive mail bought hat! Went to Mrs. Miller's card party. Studied for Sunday school further.

Oct. 11, Sun. Taught my class and heard a good sermon from the Bishop. Dinner at Mrs. Gold's. For 2 hours and 20 minutes read <u>The Nigger</u>, by Edward Sheldon, to Minna on the hill. Splendid play[23]

Oct. 14, Wed. Kept in some boys and talked most seriously to Carl and Campbell. Carl helped me carry water and brought me a gift with Allen. He's a dear. Downtown for Spanish class. Played basketball with in-town teacher's team. Wrote a letter.

Oct. 15, Thurs. After school we called on Mrs. Miller, Mrs. Ferguson and Mrs. Gardner. Georgia and I talked much of the evening. I had a rich letter day again. Heard from my Ruth.

Oct. 16, Fri. Basketball just for my room after school. Supper by the lake. Fire of cones with Mary Jane. Basketball, with town teachers team. I play forward, fun. Watched boys play.

Oct. 18, Sun. Taught my tots, then went to St. John's with Georgia and Mary Jane. Good sermon. Dinner at the Golds'. Walk with Minna and Mr. Y. Mrs. Cureton spent most of afternoon with us. Letters. Prohibition speech at M. E. Church.

Oct. 20, Tues. Still examinations and correction of papers. Had a good ride through the canyon with Willard Smith. Dinner at the Golds'. Washed some clothes.

Oct. 21, Wed. Examination week still filling time and thought. I am dishwasher this week, too. At basketball a big guard nearly wore me out. I am little!

Oct. 23, Fri. New efforts at disciplining my mischievous boys. Inspiring walk to the hill. Made candy.

---

23 Elsie's story takes place in an America that was rapidly changing. Unfortunately, it was an America that was also still steeped in strong racial and social divides. Some of the vocabulary and terms Elsie and others used reflected the all-too-common views of that time. I decided to keep them to retain authenticity, although I do not agree with their use and am glad that today such words and views are neither acceptable nor common.

Oct. 25, Sun. Sunday school, dinner at the Golds', and then from 3:30 to 6 a lovely tramp with Minnie, Pauline and Ed.

Oct. 28, Wed. We took our dinner out by the lake again. Basketball.

Oct. 30, Fri. Read to my room more than usual of Treasure Island. Went to the hill for autumn leaves for the party. Helped with refreshments and entertainment. Fun. Played ghost, howled and told weird tales.

Oct. 31, Sat. Halloween and Minna's birthday. Housework. Rode to Supai with Miss Reese. Dance at the Parish house. Home at 2:30 A.M.! A new interest!

Nov. 1, Sun. S.S. at Methodist Church. For the first time I took communion in an Episcopal church. The solemnity moved me. Helped Mary Jane feed the Mexicans. Prohibition meeting at church.

Nov. 3, Tues. Rose earlier than usual and darned stockings before school. Extra time at noon, when I voted "Arizona Dry"[24] With other teachers and interesting young men had two auto rides and one blow-out! Read Light That Failed, too sad, and not inspiring.

Nov. 6, Fri. At fifteen minutes of 3 took my children for a tramp on the hill, and enjoyed them. G. and I had a 20 mile auto trip with Pete and Miles to the K.Y. Ranch.

Nov. 7, Sat. Pete and two of the basketball boys from Flagstaff came to dinner. They didn't all understand place-cards and courses! One was from Cornville. Mary and Mr. Y., chocolates and poetry in evening.

Nov. 8, Sun. Train to Phoenix. Letter from Karl informs me he is already at Phoenix. With Marguerite we ought to have a reunion! Left Williams at 10:40 with "Youngblood family!" Whole crowd changed at Ash Fork.

Nov. 9, Mon. Phoenix. Arrived at 8:45 AM., and went to Institute. Looked in vain for one friend, but saw Marguerite and Gladys Searle, etc. One good speaker at Institute. Went to bed early.

---

24 This small town had eight saloons in 1914. On the January night before the dry law took effect, people were thick around the saloons, but at midnight all remaining liquor was poured out until the gutters ran with it. Arizona was the tenth Western state to permit women to vote; it was 1917 before Eastern states granted women that right. Elsie's vote was challenged, apparently because she was from California.

Nov. 10, Tues. Disturbed, but in the evening sent a messenger and then tried to feel better. Interesting to go about with crowd and see town.

Nov. 11, Wed. Desperate. How strange life is! Karl called in the evening for a short time, while I was at our rooming place alone. Felt better, tho still. . .

Nov. 12, Thurs. Rain over. Rose cheerful. Music at Institute again affected me. Fair with Mary Collins. Met Mr. Tatem, and went after races to see stock, etc. with him, and to dinner with him in town. Pain and amusement.

Nov. 13, Fri. Minna, Mr. Y. and I shopped, and then had lunch at fairgrounds. Wish I were. . . what? Karl hunted me up at cafe and went with Mr. Y., Minna and me to Donofrio's and to watch parade. Judge Layton chaperoned! Karl and I went to see musical comedy. A good evening. I feel unutterably more glad.

Nov. 14, Sat. Left Phoenix, once the hateful city, feeling a warm spot for it after all, despite fact that Pomona College reunion was not held there, etc.! I am thankful for blessings. Wrote 20 cards on observation car. Mary, Miss Watson, Minna, and I together having a pleasant day. Home again, with strange feelings and new resolves.

Nov. 15, Sun. Rose late, rather weary after Phoenix, but taught my tots at Sunday school. Talked and napped and wrote home and to A.M. Parker.

Box 161
Williams, Ariz.
Nov. 15, 1914

Dearest Family:

Mama, your card came while I was gone and awaited me. I received the letter in Phoenix.

We got home about 6:30 last night, after an all day trip. We left Phoenix at 7:45 A.M. and had a wait at Ash Fork late in the afternoon. It was pleasant to go through familiar places, Prescott and Jerome Junction and Cedar Glade and Ash Fork. We had seats in the Observation Coach, which meant great comfort, and splendid views of the grand scenery. There were two meals on the diner. The luxury was fun. The state pay our transportation to Institute, and also salary for the week. Of course we had extra expenses out of our own purses. Minna and I had a room (a fine sleeping-porch one) for $2.00 a night, $5 apiece for the time we were there. That of course we have to pay. Our meals at cafes were probably more than if we had been home, too, and the fair cost us something.

I'm very glad I could go. I had some delightful times. We had one speaker at Institute, Mr. Shryock, President of Illinois Normal, who alone was worth going for. Some of the speakers weren't nearly so good. There was much fine music. Mr. Youngblood, who sings tenor, gave a solo one day. We had sessions from 9 to 11:50 A. M. and from 1:10 to 4 P.M. We missed some of the section meetings at the beginnings of sessions. The meetings were all held in the Monroe School, of which I sent you a picture.

Phoenix reminded me more of Los Angeles than of Long Beach, it is such a city. Some of the scenery looked so much like Calif. it almost made me homesick. Other views, such as that from the Fair grounds, were typical of Arizona, with wild rugged peaks instead of softened ones. There were palm, pepper, fig, olive and orange trees there. Northern Arizona of course is too cold for those. But the air isn't our grand air here and we were all glad to get back to our beautiful Williams.

We got there early Monday morning since we left here at 10:30 Sunday night. Mr. Y. had engaged berths for the whole crowd, and where we changed from the main line at Ash Fork near midnight, the conductor on the Phoenix line asked if this were the "Blood family" or "Young family" who had engaged places! He must have thought Mr. Youngblood had a harem. We were more or less with some other Williams people, including the Buglens, who stayed at the Adams Hotel in Phoenix for the Fair, paying $50.00 a day for their suite! I was taken to the Monroe School in their elegant machine one day. But I think it's wicked for them to pay so much just for rooms. We were not all together in Phoenix, but Georgia and Miss Keating and Minna and I, as well as Mr. Y., were in one house where there were three rooms to rent. We were about seven blocks from town, and the other side of town from the Monroe School, so we had a good deal of exercise in walking. The rain didn't bother us much, and most of the weather was glorious, tho warm. We preferred the mud to the dust we had been told to expect. Williams seems cold now!

We got our luncheons at a cafeteria in town, and our dinners at various places. Everything was high, of course. Minna and I had taken fruit and I triscuit and raw eggs in our suitcases, so we ate our breakfasts in our room. One night Georgia and Lu Keating (one of the teachers) and I went for our supper to Donofrio's, the Sweet Shop of Phoenix. We paid 40 cents for 6 fried oysters apiece there! Excuse all this mention of prices. I thought they would interest you. We were interested in noticing everything.

Minna and Mr. Y. and I got terribly "stung" Friday noon at the Fairgrounds, when we ate at a rough oil-cloth covered table beside the gay, howling "Pike" and ordered only hamburg steak, with a bit of potato, and it was 50 cents apiece! As Mr. Y. was the only man who belongs, in a sense, to the group of 10 teachers from Williams, we made him let us pay our own way chiefly.

Monday night I was glad to take a hot bath and go to bed early. We did some shopping. I bought an umbrella ($2.00 for a cheap one) and some hose and a few gifts and Christmas cards. It was a pleasure to see the attractive store windows. Williams has some good stores, but they are few in number. The Phoenix ones were like Los Angeles. I got two of three beautiful photographs of the Grand Canyon for gifts, little booklets (4 or 5 cents apiece) for my school children for Christmas, etc. For several days we were a stupid crowd, owing partly, at least, to change of altitude.

Karl was with the rest of the University militia, 200 students, who were camped at the Fairgrounds several miles from town. I saw him at the Fair in his uniform and liked it. He was helping with the exhibits, helped judge them and was very busy. He came out for Wednesday evening, and we had a good talk. It seems incredible that this polished, clever, perfectly-groomed and fastidious University and city man is the ex-cowboy and rancher of last year! He apparently is very popular. He's working awfully hard this year, which is to be his last there and hopes to buy a bunch of cattle in Northern Arizona next year. Our relationship is just friendship now, but we are very good friends. I like his point of view, and think he is splendid.

Thursday at noon Institute closed. I saw Marguerite there, and two Pomona fellow-alumni, a Long Beach High School fellow-alumni and Ruth's one-time friend, Gladys Searle, all attending Institute.

That afternoon we went to the Fair, but as there weren't enough Grand Stand tickets already bought for our crowd to go around, Mary Collins and I were going to try to find seats just two together. We found all in the Grand Stand were taken, so like sports we got box seats. Someone thought 50,000 people were there that day. Even the box was crowded and a man Mary knew happened to see us and took us to his box. One of the other men, friends of this man's I suppose, who were in the box, was a man we had met in Williams, now Assistant State's Attorney-General. A friend of his, a Mr. Tatem, rather naturally fell to my lot. After the exciting races (auto ones that day, including Barney Oldfield)[25] Mary's friend took her and Mr. Tatem took me to see some of the stock exhibits. They were very interesting. The four of us went back to town in a machine together and then Mr. Tatem insisted on taking me to dinner. He seemed rather amusingly "smitten," if I may say so, and was much disappointed because I wouldn't stay down for all the evening with him. I did go to dinner with him, but made him take me home soon afterwards. He seemed to think he might come here to see me, so you may possibly hear of him again! We girls all thought it a huge joke. I didn't encourage him much, tho I rather liked him. He's a Phoenix man.

Friday Georgia came home. Minna and Mr. Y. and I shopped and then went to the Fair grounds. We watched the horse races a while, saw more of the exhibits, had lunch. These two aren't romantically attached, and Minna feels better if I keep them from being just "two in a crowd" sometimes. I took a rest after we came home and did some other things.

I was with Karl all the evening. Part of the time we were with Minna and Mr. Y. also. We went to Donofrio's for ice-cream after dinner and then stood on the crowded, decorated streets for an hour or two waiting for and watching the parade. Our county supt., old Judge Layton, joined us

---

25 Barney Oldfield was the first person to drive an automobile at a speed of one mile per minute. Four years earlier he had set a record with an average speed of 131 mph. Oldfield also starred in several movies, including a 1913 silent film called *Barney Oldfield's Race for a Life*, in which he races a train in order to save heroine Mabel Normand, who has been tied to the tracks by the villain.

there, and spent an hour or so with us. By the way, I saw "Pater" Miller, county supt. of Yavapai Co., at Institute and had very friendly chats with him. Judge Layton wanted to take us all to a "movie," but still other people joined the group, and after a while Karl and I just left the others with sudden adieus and went to the Columbia Theater. It is a pretty little theater, the best in town, but the show was a rather wild musical comedy, we found. We didn't get home until nearly midnight.

I hope you will have good fortune in selling turkeys, Papa. The bread is delicious toasted, Mama. Thank you very much for it. I'll write a letter about Christmas later.

Isn't the war more and more awful?[26] My check dress was a treasure in Phoenix. I wore the silk poplin, too.

With much love to each and all, Elsie

Nov. 16, Mon. Full day indeed, school better after the vacation. Teacher's meeting and girl's basketball. Then Sunday school teachers had dinner at the Methodist parsonage.

Nov. 17, Tues. Monthly exams again! Especially enjoyed the girls in folk-dances after school. Washed clothes and dishes and wrote letters, went to town with girls, called on the Watsons.

Nov. 18, Wed. Examinations, Basketball, town teachers team at seven o'clock, lots of fun.

Nov. 19, Thurs. Corrected papers after school, while little Howard Turtly called on me. Mary and Miss Barnes and Mr. Youngblood spent the evening.

Nov. 20, Fri. Worked on monthly report and folk dances and Christmas gifts. Minna and I went to the Harvey House for dinner. A year ago!

Nov. 21, Sat. Dreams of someone I first knew a year ago. Went with my children for a picnic on the cliff. Went to see University of Arizona agriculture train.

---

26 Germany had begun zeppelin raids on London. Belgians reported facing starvation. German war camps reported to have over 400,000 prisoners (*Chronicle of the 20th Century*).

Nov. 22, Sun. My tots were restless in Sunday school. Rode with Georgia and Easter Miller to Indian hieroglyphics.

Nov. 23, Mon. Too tired. Why don't I learn sense? But school went well. Read of and from Whittier to children. Heard Bishop Atwood speak on Whittier, his personal friend.

Nov. 24, Tues. Enjoyed the folk dancing afterward. Am cook for luncheons this week.

Letter from Elsie's mother
Elsinore November 24, 1914

My Dear Elsie,

So glad to get your good letter this evening. Hylinda went to town with Joe, she brought your letter.

Thanks for your Thanksgiving wishes. I too, have much to be thankful for, three fine, good daughters is among the greatest, and blessed little Dorothy, and a dear loving husband, and Aunt Mamie and above all our blessed Savior, Jesus Christ.

How fine that you expect to be able to get here Christmas eve. If you won't have to leave here before Friday I surely think Alice ought to come up, for it may be you three girls won't get together again for many years. I hope you won't give up getting a suit. Remember you must not give us Christmas gifts. Your gift to us all will be to have your own dear self here with us.

Much Love for you,
Mama

Nov. 25, Wed. Received a Thanksgiving box from home, from my dear family. Georgia had the basketball boys to dinner.

Nov. 26, Thurs. Thanksgiving Day. I gave thanks. Morning service at St John's Mission. G. and I went to the Winnans' for dinner and Minna and I walked on the hill.

Nov. 27, Fri. Party given by Mary, "mixed crowd!" Good time, roughhouse at end. Home about 1:30!

Nov. 28, Sat. Lazy, restful day, too threatening in weather to ride. Shopped with Minna. Miss Watson and Mrs. Gold called. Mended.

Nov. 29, Sun. Had my S.S. class, but stayed home from church because of my cold.

Nov. 30, Mon. School, so much still for me to learn, for the sake of the children, not in books! Basketball for my girls in the evening. I can't say what. . .

Dec.1, Tues. In the first snowstorm I had a letter from Helen Charles that tore my heart. Oh my little Ruth!

Dec. 2, Wed. A hand of stone seemed to be upon my heart. Wrote to Ruth. Dinner at Fray Marcos. Made candy. Shopped by mail.

Dec. 3, Thurs. Especially enjoyed school yesterday and to-day. Corrected papers. At home Minna gave confidences.

Dec. 4, Fri. Mr. Youngblood and Judge Layton both visited my room, and the Judge made me feel good. Minna got a telegram telling of her nephew's death. Poor girl! I went to bed supper less with an awful headache.

Dec. 5, Sat. Still some headache and a great deal of heartache. Washed, ironed and mended. I wished I could comfort Minna. Georgia read aloud in evening.

Dec. 6, Sun. Took Minna's children and mine too for Sunday school. Wrapped up a box of pine sprays I gathered for my Ruth, with many thoughts of her.

Dec. 7, Mon. Talked most solemnly to my children about evil. Oh if I could help them to be pure and true! Called on Mrs. Winans. Dinner at Fray Marcos.

Dec. 8, Tues. Still building the fires soon after 7 A.M. Cold! Ice in the tea-kettle this morning. Letter from Melissa made me dare to hope about Ruth. If only she is truly better! Earnest talk with Willard.

Dec. 9, Wed. Long teachers meeting. Dined at the Fray Marcos. I wrote to Mrs. Hurst about Christmas.

Dec.10, Thurs. A day I cannot forget. I heard the sweet news about my little sister, Alice, and was moved and glad she is expecting. I went to the Women's Club and in the evening to the movies with Mr. Connor, and dared not open a letter till he left. Then I knew that I only am left of Triumvirate. [Devastating news of Ruth's death.] May God be with me. The girls helped. In a snowstorm we took a letter for Alice M. Parker to the night train.

Letter from Ruth Stailey's cousin
Dec. 8, 1914

Dearest Elsie,
    Your dear remembrance, the pine boughs, came this afternoon just in time for Ruth to see and enjoy, for she passed on at 7:30 tonight, very quietly, and very suddenly
    Our hearts are all heavy but we are trying to know that God is our present help in time of trouble, and Auntie is bearing up bravely

Much love to you Elsie, from the family,
Ethel

Dec. 11, Fri. A strange sad day. The teachers were very good to me, and M. and G. took some of my classes. With many tears I wrote to Ruth's people, and Caroline's and mine. I found Minna and I are really friends, and that helped.

Dec. 12, Sat. The snow is beautiful, and seems to mean peace. It seems as if Ruthie can't be gone, and I still here. Oh my Ruthie!

Dec. 13, Sun. Minna took my class, and helped yet more in other ways. I am grateful for her. Bessie's letter of the night before meant much. The little white dress like mine is to be worn always by my sleeping darling. I ache at heart. I am glad she loved the pines I sent. Went with Mr. Y. to see my injured Redd boy, and with Irma to Riola's home.

Dec. 14, Mon. Alice's Special Delivery letter of understanding sympathy and love blesses me today. After school I read it yet again by the frozen lake and the snow. We went to dinner across the street again. Vera Dye and Mr. Scantlin called and asked me to come tomorrow for cards. Of course I won't go now, and she says she'll postpone it, as it was for Mr. Connor and me.

Ruth Stailey and Elsie 1913

Dec. 15, Tues. I corrected papers and wrapped up Christmas gifts. No, I cannot realize. . .

Dec. 16, Wed. The letters of sympathy and love help so very much!

Letter from Fanny Hand, a college friend
Wed. Dec. 16

Dearest Elsie,

It's no use telling you how sorry I am, for you already know, but I do wish I could do something to comfort you. If you were only here and could do something yourself, perhaps, to help Ruth's people, it would probably make it easier for you. Last summer when Freda got word of Willie Long's death in the mine she nearly went frantic because she could do nothing but sit and wait for the details which, when they came were more heart-breaking than the suspense.

I was terribly shocked at the news of Ruth's death, but I realize now that you must have been fearing that for some time. It does seem such a short time since Caroline's death, and as you say it makes the sorrow less to know that the two dear friends are together again.

Dear Elsie it must be doubly hard for you to be among strangers at this time, and yet your work is surely a blessing. Write when you feel able and tell me all that you care to. I somehow feel that if you were here you would talk to me a lot about Ruth and perhaps that would make you feel less desolate.

Elsie please take care of yourself. Your mind is altogether too intense for the strength of your body and I think that was one of Ruth's troubles. But when people are made that way it's hard to tell whether they can change.

> With love and my deepest
> sympathy from your, Fan

Dec. 17, Thurs. Georgia is sick, and we are taking care of her. Got a light dinner at home. The Golds called. The letters are still coming and blessing me. I still don't know about Oak Creek.

Dec. 18, Fri. Rather shaky; glad it is the last school day of the week. Invitations for parties for the holidays. The snow is beautiful. I am grateful for the love which blesses me in those still living and those gone on.

Dec. 19, Sat. Full day of work, washed clothes, did some housecleaning, went to two rehearsals, etc. Letter from Helen Charles told more of my dear Ruth.

Dec. 20, Sun. Loved my tots at Sunday School. Wrote to Ruth's George and other friends of hers, and mine, and her family. Phoned Mrs. Hurst.

Dec. 21, Mon. Decorated with garlands of evergreen, helped by my dear children. Then they helped me buy gifts and wrap them for each other. Bought patterns for baby clothes! Plans for Oak Creek.

Dec. 22, Tues. The pipes of the school furnace burst so no more school. My room celebrated after school, drawing gifts from the decorated basket. Hilarious fun. We trimmed our tree at home, and opened gifts. My dear family!

Dec. 23, Wed. Finished report cards and cleaned house in morning. Some of my children gave me gifts, Preparations for trip.

Dec. 24, Thurs. Cornville, Oak Creek. Met Mr. Hurst at Cedar Glade. Rufus Hill met me at Clarkdale, aching ride. Oak Creek and "Home Sweet Home." The dear tots at the entertainment, and then the Hursts.

Dec. 25, Fri. Helped the babies [Karl's little sisters Harriet and Edna] dress and play, and saw their joy over their tree. My own gifts. Mrs. Hurst and I talked intimately. She showed me Karl's baby and little boy pictures.

Dec. 26, Sat. I love the dear children. I helped Mrs. H. and danced with Ruth and played croquet. Moonlight on the creek!

Dec. 27, Sun. Shadyvale Ranch. The children of mine again at S.S. Came home with the Girdners. Talked Pomona with Miss Beck and loved Eva. Alone I saw the lights in the shack at night. Sunday evening there.

Dec. 28, Mon. The Hursts'. Lunch at the shack with Eva and Miss Beck. Pineapple and a lizard in it! The creek and memories. Rufus Hill came for me. The dance. Home at a quarter to four A. M.

Jerome News, January 8, 1915
CORNVILLE

One of the prettiest dances of the holiday season was held in the Oak Creek Schoolhouse on Monday evening. The night was almost perfect for traveling and the young people came from distant places to engage in their devotions to Terpsichore until the wee small hours. The music was excellently rendered by Mr. and Mrs. Johnson, Mr. and Mrs. J. O. Hurst and Miss Alta Van Deren. Among those present from nearby points were: J. G. Van Deren and wife, Mr. and Mrs. Chestnut, Mable Lee, Elsie Hayes, Dollie and Iva Van Deren, Mary Stofin, Ocie Raleston, Myrtle Van Deren, Mrs. Eulalia Bourne[27], Misses Collins, Ada, Hazel, and Grace Danna, Dick Mason, Lloyd

---

27 In *Ranch Schoolteacher* Eulalia Bourne wrote, "I was fired for dancing the one-step. I had been warned. Everybody on the creek had heard about the new dance the Yale boys had taught Ruby and me the summer before at Griscom's. There were rumors that it was improper, even vulgar. It was called 'the rag' or 'jazz'—a dirty word in that time and place. Ruby and I thought it new and fascinating. The dance-floor manager was a tall, long-faced blond fellow, obviously a farm worker. At the beginning he announced that this was to be strictly a decent dance. There would be no 'rag,' no 'jazz.'"

Van Deren, Frank Owenby, Chester Willard, Bill Gray, George Dickerson, Lester Mickle, Henry Stofin, Paul Tissau, Alex Willard, Bill Cook, Will and Pete Schroder, Will Chestnut, Bill Back, Myron Loy, Lynn Derrick, Irving Walker, Harvey Thurston, John Fredericks, Dave and Jim Hopkins and Jim Hazel.

Dec. 29, Tues. Talked with Mrs. Hurst, yet more intimately. I won't forget this day.

Dec. 30, Wed. "Wash Day," and I am allowed to help. Walked with the family. Pictures drawn for stories told to Edna and Harriett. Pile of mail.

Article from the Cottonwood newspaper:

Mrs. John O. Hurst entertained on Thursday afternoon in honor of her guest, Miss Elsie Hayes of Williams. Miss Hayes was a former teacher at this place and chief among the guests were her former pupils. The party assembled on the well-kept lawn and devoted the glorious winter afternoon hours to croquet and swinging. Later popcorn and homemade candies were served. Mrs. Edgar Page rendering some delightful music meanwhile. Several snapshots of the group on the green lawn were taken. Mrs. Hurst's home is in a sheltered nook at the foot of House mountain and the lawn of Kentucky blue grass is as luxuriant and green as though its roots were buried deep in the fertile soil of its native state.

Dec. 31, Thurs. My Oak Creek children came for a party, and I loved them anew.

> "Is memory most of miseries miserable,
> Or the one flower of ease in bitterest hell?"
> [Dante Rosetti, "Memory"]

On one subject I write little and think much. "Silence is eloquent." What did twelve weeks bring?

Jan. 1, 1915[28] Fri. Oak Creek. We went to the Windmill, an 18 mile drive, for dinner. In the evening Mrs. Hurst and I had our final talk. May wisdom and courage come to me. May I ask for Joy?

Jan 2, Sat. Williams. Said good-bye to the Hursts and Oak Creek with regret. Rufus Hill drove me to Clarkdale. Wrote "thank you" notes on the train. Dick Connor got on at Ash Fork, so we had quite a talk. Good to have Dewdrop Inn to come to again!

Jan 3, Sun. Had my S. S. class of tots. Wrote letters and went to the Harvey House with Minna. Thought of my Ruth and of someone else.

Jan. 4, Mon. A long day School again. "Work is a boon." I feel strongly once more. It snowed. Letter writing after school, and talk with Willard.

Jan. 5, Tues. I wish. . . a year ago! Felt ill all day, from the strain of the last month, I know. Ruthie went four weeks ago. Dear letter from Bessie at night. Read In the Twinkling of an Eye, given by Hylinda.

Jan. 6, Wed. Felt better physically, and mentally too. Did extra school work until almost sick.

Jan. 7, Thurs. Worked after school and wrote letters. Read Adonais, in Alice's Shelley sent me for my comfort. I will be more cheerful and work harder!

Jan. 8, Fri. Talked about history of England at school, showing pictures. Washed clothes. Hard day, truly.

Jan. 9, Sat. Noise from broken water pipes kept me awake last night, but when I did sleep I had comforting dreams. Rose with new determination. Washed many more clothes. Callers.

Jan. 10, Sun. Read The Purple Stockings. Refused to go to a "concert" and a movie party too. In the evening wrote very late a special letter to Karl. Relieved. Played my last Card!

---

28 January 1, 1915, began prohibition in Arizona. In Thomas Marshall's booklet, "The First Six Months of Prohibition in Arizona," he noted, "Those who knew Williams in the early days can scarcely recognize it now without its saloons and drunken men lounging about the streets." His conclusion of this small book said, "Prohibition has wiped out 444 saloons in Arizona."

7

Haunting the Post Office

"Don't dare confide in my
diary how I really feel
... Eager for mail."

Elsie's "last card" revealed that she had made a final decision about Karl. With the decision came relief, probably from all those months of indecision. Still, memories seemed to haunt her, as thoughts of Ruth and Karl merged. She must have feared losing Karl as she had lost her other dear friends. Even in her diary, Elsie seemed unable to reveal her true feelings.

Jan. 11, 1915 Mon. Enjoyed school more than for a long time. Had a letter from Karl!

Jan. 12, Tues. Teachers "Sew Club" organized. Read story of Count of Monte Cristo to 7th grade. Went to see The Dollar Mark, (seen once with Ruth) at movies, followed by Santa Fe Concert.[29] Thought and thought.

Jan. 13, Wed. Don't dare confide in my diary how I really feel! Began reading The Inside of the Cup.

Jan. 15, Fri. Worked further on papers and reports. Told children about college life. Eager for mail. Finished Inside of the Cup, it is splendid, and steadies my faith in religious things.

Jan. 16, Sat. Rather calmer today, Beautiful snowstorm! Cleaned house, mended, ironed, cut out baby-kimono, shopped by mail. Remember a year ago!

Jan. 17, Sun. The dear tots at S. S., and then I went to church. Liked the new rector, Mr. Boone, and the service uplifted me. Minna and I talked, and walked in the snow. Wish I could help her! Letters, some from Mrs. Hurst and Alice. Read two of Yalsworthy's plays.

Jan. 18, Mon. Enjoyed school. Called on Mrs. Robinson, the Sines, Miss Sughrue, Mrs. Kerwan. Our pipes burst again! Snow is glorious. Still haunt Post office.

---

29 "The Santa Fe booked entertainment from across the United States and as far away as Canada and Europe. Entertainers performed in exchange for free travel to whatever destination they preferred along the Santa Fe line. Crowds for these free weekly events were often so large that Santa Fe Railroad employees and their families were seated first, with all remaining seats open to the general public just before each performance began. Shows were later performed at the Harvey House." (Richard Melzer, *Fred Harvey Houses of the Southwest* [Charleston, SC: Arcadia Press, 2008])

Jan. 19, Tues. Called on Mrs. Miller with Minna. Went with a "crowd" to see The Lure, about white slave traffic. To Harvey House.

Jan. 20, Wed. Some struggles at school with wayward children, but I love them all. Mr. Y. came and we discussed school work for next year.

Jan. 21, Thurs. Theater party and dance given for Mr. Hughes and his bride. Elegant. Enjoyed some of it very much. Saw my gifts from my dear family. It is now after two, so really my birthday. Resolutions!

Jan. 22, Fri. A brighter day for my spirit. Strong Resolutions. Enjoyed school. My children came for a party, and overwhelmed me with beautiful gifts. Hilarious time. Their love made me glad.

Jan. 23, Sat. Washed a few clothes, swept the house, mended, read, wrote letters, shopped and marketed. Thankful.

Jan. 24, Sun. My last Sunday with dear little Howard Turtly present. I like the new rector at St. John's Mission. The service blest me. Wrote many letters and cards. Finished Yalsworthy's Strife.

Jan. 25, Mon. Lu Keating and I stayed overnight at the Curetons'. Waded snow in an almost blizzard. Card from a Williams man and gossip about him at once made me disgusted and more, not the card! Read aloud to Lu some of Trelawney of the Wells. Heard Miles say his "now I lay me!"

Jan. 26, Tues. Beautiful snow, misty view of the peaks as we walked back to town to school. Enjoyed school, and work with the girls in gymnasium afterward, especially Read some literature Mrs. Darling is sending Mrs. Hurst through me.

Jan. 27, Wed. Sent some boys to Mr. Youngblood. Worked after school, and then talked with teachers, and listened to Victrola. Shopped by mail.

Jan. 28, Thurs. School. This is my "cook week." My children, led by Leroy, are "on a tear." Wrote letters.

Jan. 29, Fri. Almost a blizzard, beautiful! Sent my Bad Boy home, worn out by him. Played on piano after school. Too tired to make candy at the Golds'. Read more in Shelley. Inspiring.

Jan. 30, Sat. "Worn to a frazzle." Did some housework, cleaned ink spots etc., and was lazy. Read <u>Riders of the Purple Sage</u> by Zane Gray, whoever that is!

Jan. 31, Sun. Lazy still through wisdom. Went to the Golds' for dinner. Mary C. copied some of my "mottoes." Read <u>Quo Vadis</u>, skipping some parts.

Feb. 1, Mon. Felt physically better, and went to school. After the strain, no wonder I was tired a day or two. Went coasting with one small boy, and helped two others throw wood into our porch. Wrote to some of my Oak Creek children.

Feb. 2, Tues. Wind and mist as well as driving snow. Went alone as usual for the evening mail.

Feb. 3, Wed. Woke to find my voice gone. Gave written lessons, writing orders on board. The Sewing Club met at Mary Collins, and put patches on little overalls and mended stockings for the Mexicans. I left soon after dinner.

Feb. 4, Thurs. School, talked most seriously to Campbell and Carl, "moral 'suasion" when I thought of the strap. It seemed to do good. Went to bed early.

Feb. 5, Fri. Voice still better. Good lot of mail. Helen is so lovely and inspiring! I think much of my family. Received <u>Paola & Francesca</u> from Alice M. Parker and reread it, wonderful. Rector and family called.

Feb. 6, Sat. I washed and ironed some clothes, and rested a great deal to recover from my cold and weariness. Read <u>Francesca da Rimini</u>, which I am to review. Few books so show wild love.

Feb. 7, Sun. Tiny Vivian climbed into my lap while I told a story at S. S., and lay there quite still, restless as she is. After the sentence prayer when she lifted her head she said, "I wasn't asleep!" Wrote letters and went skiing. That was fun but social life needs adjustment here!!!

Feb. 8, Mon. Examinations again. Bought and addressed valentines. Letter from Ruth's George hurt.

Feb. 9, Tues. Used the strap, with regrets, on Carl. Finished reading a wild spirit story to the children. Gymnasium class.

Feb. 10, Wed. Examinations still. Fine letters from home. Sent A.M.P. lovely pine branches. Went to a party at Mrs. Miller's.

Feb. 11, Thurs. Day of difficult discipline at school. Kept three boys until six! Early to bed. I remember a year ago.

Feb. 12, Fri. Lincoln Program. Valentines. Bertha Peet's slumber party, seven there for overnight, teachers, and the Dye girls for evening. Taffy, popcorn, music, pranks, dancing. Really fun.

Feb. 13, Sat. A late elaborate breakfast which we helped to prepare. Elegant card party given by Mrs. Lowe.

Feb. 14, Sun. Enjoyed church service. Spent the afternoon with the girls and Mr. Y. at the Polson's, the son at home! Music. Talked at Epworth League.

Feb. 15, Mon. Enjoyed school especially. Heard the Women's Club give selections from <u>Faust</u> at the Parish House.

Feb. 16, Tues. Worked on report cards in the evening, and wrote a letter.

Feb. 17, Wed. Went to Ash Wednesday service with Mary. Lenten Resolutions. "Manlove" impersonator, made us laugh afterward.[30]

Feb. 19, Fri. As Friday's special topic talked to the children about Rome, and showed them my book. In the entertainment, their dialogue, they "did me proud."

Feb. 20, Sat. Mended, washed and ironed handkerchiefs, did errands, etc. Six of us girls, escorted by Mr. Bugeley, watched the dance and had a feast at "The Harvey."

Feb. 21, Sun. Sleepy, after going to bed about two last night! Had only two children at S. S. out of all Minna's and mine. Deep snow, through which we ploughed. Letters and callers. Early to bed.

Feb. 23, Tues. Refused to go with Dick Connor to the special movie

---

30 "The ever-popular impersonator Halwood Manlove began his circuit Chautauqua career in 1910, 'A man of many faces'…Centered his attention of his act on ethnic impersonations. Manlove carries with him a full line of grease paints, wigs and make-up materials and with the aid of these changes very quickly into Irishman, Swede, Jew, old man, tramp, dude and whatnot." John E. Tapia, *Circuit Chautauqua* (North Carolina: McFarland, 1996).

because of my children's party. Had a lot of fun with them at the Montgomerys'. Invited to go on a sleigh ride.

Feb. 24, Wed. Began reading <u>Aucassin and Nicolette</u> to the children as <u>Legend of Sleepy Hollow</u> finished. Worked on my paper for Women's Club. Repudiated sleigh ride. Went to Lenten service with Mary, and Dick Conner came home with me and called.

Feb. 25, Thurs. Gave my review of D'Annunzio's <u>Francesca da Rimini</u> before the Women's Club. Enjoyed it. Snow still. Beautiful!

Feb. 26, Fri. Showed my children pictures of California and the West in general, and talked about the Exposition. Wrote paper on my review which Mrs. Cureton wanted to go in the <u>Williams News</u>.

Feb. 27, Sat. Housework. Large sewing party at the Carlsons'. Miss Reese (?) spent the evening with us, and told us she is Mrs. Charlebois! Exciting.[31]

Feb. 28, Sun. Stayed in bed until noon, trying to get over my cold. Dinner at the Golds'. Supper with Dick Connor at Fray Marcos. He spent the evening.

March 1, Mon. School, of course. Wrote letters and now going early to bed. Whirling snowstorms.

March 2, Tues. Went with D. Connor to see <u>The Mystery of Edwin Drood</u>, very good, horrors though. Talked around fire afterward.

March 3, Wed. Announced Nita's wedding, with wedding bell, etc. at dinner of Sewing Club, my turn. We hemmed napkins for her.

March 4, Thurs. Too much "all in" with my cold and late hours to stay all night at Mrs. Cureton's. Lu and I went for afternoon committee meeting there, though driven through snow. Scarlet fever scare at school. Read <u>My Friend from India</u>.

March 5, Fri. After school did weekend housework. Cards and sewing and tales of horror in the dark.

---

31 It was probably against the rules for teachers to marry.

March 6, Sat. Rose late, a group of us served at Lu's, and had very good things to eat! The Golds had cowboys at dinner!

March 7, Sun. (Dorothy Alice arrived!) Only four tots at Sunday School this weather. Read to girls essays from <u>Atlantic Monthly</u> and <u>Century</u> sent by Mrs. Darling. Sun on snow beautiful.

March 8, Mon. Examinations again. Leroy is back. We began taking our noon meal at the Gold's. Good sunshine! Movies, then splendid Santa Fe concert.

March 9, Tues. Problems at school. Still lovely sunshine. I am cook for the suppers this week. Went with Dick Connors to see <u>When Broadway Was a Trail</u> in movies. Ordered plays for Club.

March 10, Wed. Found that I have a little niece, and I am so glad I can't express the joy. Wrote to Alice and Ernest, and the new grandparents.

March 10, 1915
My Darling Mother, Grandmother!

Your letter came this morning to me. I found it on my desk 20 minutes of 9 A.M. Oh, I am so happy about it! I rushed into the assembly, where I wasn't likely to be disturbed, and just cried!

I hope Alice and Ernest and you and all are glad it's a girl. I am. I think because they're cuter while they're wee. If I won't hug baby Myra to pieces at dinnertime this noon! To think, Alice, our youngest, is a mother! Ernest certainly is a young father! Oh, I am so glad you were there! I had been dreading it for you, tho, for I know it was terribly hard for you to stand by. I've been a bit worried, though, because I'm so far away, and I surely am relieved as well as so very, very glad. I believe it was Sunday noon that Pete, who's been in the P.O. and who often brings our mail, came to the Gold's while we were at dinner, and I imagined it might be a special delivery letter for me, and was excited until I heard him ask for Mr. Youngblood. What will she be called? I hope she'll be named soon, or is already, for she'll seem more like a person then. Do tell me everything about her, and about dearest Alice, too. How long will Alice be at the hospital? I hope you and

Ernest will be allowed there a great deal. How you'll love to care for the baby when you can. My, I wish I could be there now!

I had wondered what would happen if the time came when the play was going on, and am so glad it wasn't. Will you stay at the house and get Ernest's meals? To think you and Papa are grandparents!

I've always felt Aunt Mamie was cheated out of something because she couldn't be near Catherine and Douglas while they were tiny, and I know she'll delight in this grandniece, her first. Can't someone take care of the ranch a few days so when Papa comes for you Aunt Mamie and Hylinda can come, too?

I hope I'll hear again later in the day or tomorrow, but suppose of course everything will be all right from what you say. The letter may have come last night but tho I'd expected to get it on the way to the "movie". Dick Connor said he thought there wasn't time after we got downtown. The P.O. closes at eight, too.

The pictures were very good—5 reels—one play, a colonial story, When Broadway Was a Trail.

Monday night I went with Minna to the picture show in order to have a good seat before the free Santa Fe entertainment began. It was a splendid concert, two violins, a cello, harp, drum, and piano. I must close in haste.

With Dearest Love, Elsie

March 11, Thurs. Learned that my little niece is "Dorothy Alice Burley" and like the name. Miss James visited my room during exams (Mrs. Miller yesterday). Went to Women's Club, Ibsen's plays, and Peer Gynt music! Went to "Dick's" millinery opening.

March 12, Fri. Finished reading Aucassin at school. Enjoy getting supper at night.

March 13, Sat. Bought one of "Dick's" hats from New York, a fussy one, also a silk petticoat! Sewed and wrote and read letters. Went to Lu's to hear My Friend from India read, as we are to give it.

March 14, Sun. Beautiful sunshine! Spent the lazy sort of day I was in the mood for. Wrote many letters on back porch in sun, strolled with girls a little; read and chose choice bits from New York Times to send to friends.

March 15, Mon. Enjoyed the spring that is melting the snow in our yards. Went with Dick to Gamble Concert, splendid. Afterward to Harvey House.

March 16, Tues. Enjoyed sunshine. Wrote letters, and went rather early to bed.

March 17, Wed. Sewing Club. Met at Bertha Peet's. Afterward went to Catholic dance, and enjoyed most of it very much.

March 18, Thurs. Oh, so sleepy! M. Johnson, Lava Sughrue, Mary Jane and Miss Stanley called.

March 19, Fri. Cleaned house after school. Mary stayed overnight, and in the evening I read to her and Georgia.

March 20, Sat. All kinds of household work, mending, etc. Theater party as farewell to Minna Johnson.

March 21, Sun. Took little Anita to her home after S. S. Visited with Nita, who stayed with us last night.

March 22, Mon. School was very interesting. We hear of a new candidate for trustee, and try not to worry! My gray poplin arrived and baby hot water bottle for Dorothy. First rehearsal of My Friend from India.

March 23, Tues. Began reading Tyolet to children, but they are too sophisticated to appreciate it! Saw Lola in movies, tragic. A poor "Santa Fe." Went with Dick to Harvey House for supper.

March 24, Wed. Went to a sewing affair, and supper served by Methodists, at the Carlsons'. Called on Nita with Lu, finding Minna and Bertha there, second supper! Play rehearsal.

March 24, 1915

Dearest Mother,

Your card came yesterday, and a note from Aunt Mamie, with letters from you enclosed. I am so glad to hear all you tell! I was glad to know you were getting safely moved, and hope the new home will be very satisfactory. Don't work too hard, please! I know you enjoy it, but I am afraid you may be too tired already. I should think it would in some ways be easier not to be living at so many different places now. How good Aunt Gertie and Helen have been to help!

Dorothy must be getting more cunning all the time! How I do want to see her! The wee hot water bottle will be sent with this, I hope.

Monday night we had a first rehearsal of our play. It was more reading, but we are supposed to know the first act tonight. We didn't stay late Monday.

Last night I went with Dick to the "pictures" and the Santa Fe concert afterward. We went to the Harvey House before we were through. I had hot chocolate and chicken sandwiches there.

I wrote to Aunt Mamie Sunday and asked her to send the letter on to you. Your letter came, with the D.M.C. cotton. Thank you, very much. I've been on yard duty today, so have been particularly busy. It was grand in the sunshine. This is real spring weather. We have hall duty once a week and shall have yard duty once in two weeks now. I hope to write a longer letter next time, expected to send more of one today.

With much love to you all, Elsie

March 25, Thurs. Troubles at school. Sent Jose home. Still excitement over coming school elections. Review of <u>Chanticleer</u> at Women's Club. Got the baby hot water bottle and the wee wrapper I made ready to go to Dorothy. Rehearsal.

March 26, Fri. Told the children about the Orient in special period. A group of us walked to dam, overflowing and beautiful. Mr. Twitty took us out in machine. Real spring! Embroidered.

March 27, Sat. I washed some clothes and my hair, did housework, mending and errands in town. Talked with Minna. Nita for all night.

March 28, Sun. Sunday school and church. Rested in my room the rest of the day. Wrote to Mother and another letter I may not send.

March 28, 1915, Sunday

Dearest Mother,

Spring has really come here. Buds are bursting, the sun shining, the snow melting faster than ever.

I went to Sunday school and church this morning, and have been lazy the rest of the day. Please excuse writing, as I'm curled up in bed now. It is evening, and the girls have gone to church.

Nita stayed with us again last night. Got in about 10:30 after a day of hunting, and seemed to appreciate a warm house, hot bath and bed awaiting her. Her husband is expected now in a week or so from Phoenix or the vicinity. He's a sheep man. She's still teaching. Mary has been here a great deal evenings and other times. Lu drops in quite often, too, and some other people.

The eggs are so fresh and good! I was delighted to get them, so many, too!

You must enjoy bathing the baby. I should think it would be hard for you to have to get up so many times in the night to see to her. If Aunt Mamie thinks the auto trip would be too hard for her don't you suppose she might go soon by train? I hope she, too, can see Dorothy soon.

We have March winds a good deal. One is blowing now.

Mr. Hughes was elected yesterday as the new trustee. Probably none of us will be "fired" now unless it's Mr. Youngblood. He's had some trouble with the janitor, but the teachers will surely be disgusted if he's fired. He's being slandered, too, but those who know him think he is really unusually "good", in other words, moral. The gossiping that goes on in this town is awful!

A few days ago Dr. Jeffries, who lives across the street from us, stopped me on the street and said with a broad grin, "Well, I suppose we'll soon be hearing the announcement of your engagement to Dick Connor!" I certainly was disgusted.

We are having play rehearsals three times a week now. We are supposed to know our parts in the first act tomorrow night. It is good fun. All the women's parts are taken by teachers, Lu, Nita, Mary, Georgia and myself. Lu is coaching it. There are several married men and several unmarried ones in it, well known business men of Williams. A number of them happen to be in the choir of St. John's Mission (the Episcopal Church).

I am returning the clipping about Ernest. It surely sounds well. I am eager to see the Mission Play again, with him in it. I wish I could hear him on Easter. How I would love to see Alice with Dorothy!

With much love to you, and all, Elsie

March 29, Mon. Went to Nita's for supper. Play rehearsal where I found I have a new fiancé.

March 30, Tues. Dick Connors asked me to go to see "the pictures," but we had a long rehearsal, so I didn't go.

March 31, Wed. Carl Downey lovable but naughty, said good-bye. I helped Nita with her dinner for the Sewing Club.

April 1, Thurs. Thought of special day[32] Simple Arbor Day preparations. Got supper, and talked with Minna, bless her!

April 2, Fri. Good Friday and Arbor Day. Glorious tramp by the dams. Good Friday service. After program (when my children were horrid) we had a holiday. Letter from Cornville trustees asking me to apply there because the "little kids" want me so much! [Elsie cherished that letter, though she was surprised by the informal lined paper.]

Cornville, Arizona
March 30, 1915

Dear Miss Hayes,

I will write to you regarding our next term of school. While we like Miss Beck very much as a teacher, but in the estimation of the little kids there seems to be no one quite the equal to Miss Hayes in their opinion, and they are all of the same opinion. Therefore we as trustees would be glad to consider your application for the primary room for our next term. We expect to retain Miss Finnie as provided if she wants the place so far as I know at present, although she has not applied.

---

32 Karl's birthday, now almost three months since she had heard from him.

Hope to hear from you at an early date and oblige yours truly,

> John H. Lee, trustee district 16
> P.S. Our school is at present
> closed on account of measles.
> Those that have them are Hursts,
> Duncans, Stricks, and Lees.

April 3, Sat. Day of "Manual Labor!" Washed some clothes, cleaned house, helped Minna decorate for Methodist services. Mourned for Ruth at night. Minna helped me.

April 4, Sun. Easter Day. Candy eggs hidden for S. S. tots. Splendid letter from Alice M. Parker. Long Easter communion service at St. John's mission blessed me deeply. Thought much of Ruth.

April 5, Mon. School work kept me late, then took flowers from Methodists to Mrs. Joiner, my dear little Anita's mother. Sent flowers for Riola's grandfather's funeral. Dick made a long call.

Teachers dressed for "manual labor"

April 6, Tues. Went up the hill several times to help look after Nita, who is suddenly ill. Had an interview with a new trustee arranged by Dick! Play practice instead of moving pictures.

April 7, Wed. Wish I could be home, with Alice and Dorothy there now! Good play practice.

April 8, Thurs. Still examinations. Women's Club after school, The Joy of Living, Sudermann reviewed by Lu. Called to see Nita. Corrected papers and wrote cards to Oak Creek children.

April 9, Fri. Went to the children's operetta, The Brownies Whispers, and helped behind the scenes. Very pretty

April 10, Sat. Tried to spend the day restfully. Dinner at the Charlebois'. Beautiful horseback ride with Pauline Jones.

April 11, Sun. Such dear, funny tots at S.S.! Wrote letters, and went regretfully to rehearsal at Sultana. Read Last Days of Pompeii and the Quarterly

April 12, Mon. The Prayer Book came to me which seven years ago I gave to my Ruthie, and with it pictures she left marked for me. My tears have come, but I feel her nearness.

April 13, Tues. Worked on reports after school until almost six. Fine bunch of letters! Went with Dick to see The Marked Woman, a "Santa Fe," and to the Harvey

April 14, Wed. After an hour at school came home, sick with "acute indigestion," according to Dr. Melick. Miserable day!

April 15, Thurs. Mrs. Barclay took my work at school. Felt better, and read short stories, Waverley, etc. Mrs. Phillips and Mrs. Winans called, as well as girls.

April 16, Fri. Sat by kitchen fire most of the day, reading sermons, magazines, and Waverley! Still weak, or would be at school.

April 17, Sat. Got up at noon, and did some work; but chiefly was "lazy." Talked much with Minna. I enjoy her deeply

April 18, Sun. "Williams" still! Wrote letters, and read with delight Atlantic

Monthly and in <u>The Supremacy of Jesus</u>. Enjoyed sunset. Callers, restful time.

April 19, Mon. Good to be at school again. Feel far better. My children said nice things to me. Shopped, talked with girls, got supper.

April 20, Tues. Reading <u>Last Days of Pompeii</u> to children. Read Muhlbach's <u>Berlin</u> and <u>Sans-Souci</u>, love-stories. Brief rehearsal. Lester now is my third fiancé!

April 21, Wed. Enjoyed "yard duty" at school. Had a hard time managing Leroy. Shopped and got "dinner."

April 22, Thurs. Went with Dick to a fussy party at the Dyes'. Place blue with smoke! In bed seven minutes of two.

April 23, Fri. Put flowers from California all over the house, went downtown. I chose dress goods.

April 24, Sat. Washed and ironed some clothes, and then sat in the sun and wrote letters. Nita came for overnight, and we sewed.

April 25, Sun. Rehearsal in morning. Ralph Johnson is my fourth fiancé of the play!

April 26, Mon. Worked hard at school. Talked all evening. Miss Stanley for supper.

April 27, Tues. Pleasant day of friendliness with everybody. After school went to Bertha Peet's and downtown with little Edward Dewey.

April 28, Wed. Pleasant evening for the Sewing Club at Miss Watson's. Sewed on towel for Nita. Rain.

April 29, Thurs. Heavy snow! Signed my contract for next year, $1,000. Dreams the last nights I cannot forget. I think of Ruth.

April 30, Fri. Icy blizzard to welcome May! Took flowers to my sick Minnie. Funny Minstrel show with the girls.

May 1, Sat. Fourteen inches of snow on the level for May Day, and falling all day to make that depth! Cleaned house.

May 2, Sun. Still snowing. Rehearsal. Lovely afternoon by fire, with Minna. Long letters from and to Alice. Baby Myra and ice-cream.

May 3, Mon. Beginning examinations again. Went to Oriental party at Methodist Church.

May 4, Tues. Went through the snow for pine-boughs for Mamie, and found nature gloriously inspiring.

May 5, Wed. Word from "G.E.M.H." [Gertrude Harnett, one of Caroline Harnett's sisters], with picture of house at 10th and Locust, Long Beach, wrung my heart with memories. I can hardly wait to be with "them that knows me," as Edna once said. Oh Ruth!

May 6, Thurs. At 7:35 A.M. saw Mary Harter and her family for ten good minutes! I have felt rich all day. Went down through snow. It makes me hurt, too. Took flowers to Riola who is sick.

May 7, Fri. Two years ago went on 1913 class picnic in Cucamonga Canyon, and roamed with Deak. One year ago went to Claremont! Can hardly wait for school to be out.

May 8, Sat. Deposited my salary, bathed, rested, went to call on Mrs. Kenneth Hughes, girls here to supper, rehearsal until 11:30.

May 9, Sun. Full day, though different from a year ago! Minna is at Ash Fork, so I took her S. S. class with mine. Rushed home and donned a middy, and went to picnic in beautiful canyon including snowballing. Three hour rehearsal.

May 10, Mon. Still particularly busy at school. Took a short rest and baked sweet potatoes and cooked rice with tomato. Went to the schoolhouse for a rehearsal. It was a hilarious one this time!

May 11, Tues. Glorious sunshine! Walked with the girls to see the Peaks. Little Mexicans pelted us with flowers and grass! Harvey House for pie, and May here for rest of supper. Saw <u>Deep Purple</u> with crowd of teachers.

May 12, Wed. Voice almost lost again! Minna's turn to have the Sewing Club to dinner.

May 13, Thurs. Mrs. Phillips visited school again. Wind. Wrote to Helen, planning Commencement. Packed my suitcase for the Canyon.

May 14, Fri. Special work at school. Rested and decided to buy $90.00

Elsie visited Hopi Point Lookout, one of three fire towers constructed by the US Forest Service on the rim of the Grand Canyon. USFS photo, 1909.

worth of "scrip." [Scrip was a certificate to be exchanged for goods, as at a company store.] Rehearsal.

May 15, Sat. Grand Canyon. Words about this place are weak and useless. Minna and I had a wonderful day that began when we left at 4 A.M. Mr. Smiley took charge of us, hotel full. Walked about rim to Hopi Point. Visited with a scientist and Forest Service man. Indian dance, etc. with railroad people.

May 16, Sun. Williams. Another wonderful day. At five saw sunrise over the Canyon. Picnic breakfast at Hopi Point. The tower of the Forest Service again. Luncheon at El Tovar. [El Tovar hotel was built in 1905 and was one of the grandest hotels in the West.] Leisurely afternoon, at Lookout, etc. Last looks at the vastness near sunset. Met by Mr. Youngblood at 10:10 at Williams. I shall always be better for the Canyon.

May 17, Mon. Tried to be philosophical over a "teacher's trouble." Discovered my scrip book was lost. Went at night to station in the rain.

May 18, Tues. I remember a year ago! Note of apology from a pupil's mother cleared the air. Long and late rehearsal.

May 19, Wed. A year ago Alice was married. Today it snowed and snowed. My scrip book is found!

May 20, Thurs. Chaperoned some of my children to a concert, glorious. Creatore's Band. Enjoyed it all.

May 21, Fri. Enjoyed school particularly. Play rehearsal at Sultana until almost midnight.

May 22, Sat. Heard Aunt Mamie is sick, and wish I were home. Callers. Sorted and packed. Rehearsal. My pretty new dress came from my dear mother.

May 23, Sun. If only today I could hear from Ruth; and write to her, as always before for today! [Anniversary of Caroline's death in 1907.] I took her Prayer Book to church communion, which blest me. Sunday school, rehearsal, letters, early to bed.

May 25, Tues. Borrowed an evening gown with train. Called on the Watsons. Saw Lillian Russell in <u>Wildfire</u> at Sultana in "pictures," then sleepy rehearsal there.

May 26, Wed. Began final examinations. Went to Ladies Aid Supper at Mrs. Drennans'. Rested. Rehearsed at schoolhouse.

May 27, Thurs. Saw to costumes, etc. Went to rehearsal at a quarter to ten, home at one. Thought of my mother particularly today.

8

News Worse than Death

"Today I heard news worse than death. I can only pray. Had to keep going."

Five months had passed since Elsie had written, and received no answer to, her "last card" letter. Though she was disturbed by Karl's lack of response, nothing had prepared Elsie for the shock that awaited her. Elsie's diary did not reveal exactly what this tragic news was. It was only when I was doing research in 1988 and came across a news article that I made the surprising discovery. Elsie must have heard the news from Mrs. Hurst.

Friends and activities filled her time but not her thoughts. As Elsie plodded through these long months she continued her diary entries but her zest for life had waned. The absence of favorite words such as "glorious" and "splendid" indicated that an element of her life was missing.

May 28, 1915, Fri. Today I heard news worse than death. I can only pray. Had to keep going. We gave <u>My Friend from India</u> at night.

Prescott Journal-Miner News
Sunday Morning, May 9, 1915

Young Hurst is committed to the asylum, losing his mind because of a mysterious love affair is the belief. Hurst, who suffered under the delusion that his father was going to kill him and the rest of the family, consisting of a mother and two small girls, at a session of the superior court held last night to accommodate Judge Smith who leaves for Tucson today, was committed to the state asylum for the insane at Phoenix on the recommendation of the examining physicians, H. T. Southworth and J. R. McNally.

After a few days observation the doctors decided young Hurst, who is but 23 years old, was not responsible for his actions and would be safer behind the doors of an asylum. It is believed that his troubles are caused by some mysterious love affair. His step-father and mother declare that for the last two months he has acted very strangely and while out in the fields on his parents' farm near Cornville in the upper Verde, would stand for hours at a time blankly staring at the ground.

Hurst will be taken south in charge of a deputy sheriff this afternoon.

May 29, Sat. A strange day after a hard night.

May 30, Sun. Church helped me. Went to the Curetons' with Minna. Slept in the afternoon.

May 31, Mon. Went to picnic and party at the Robinsons', large, pretty affair. Extra schoolwork and packing.

June 1, Tues. Tired and trying to be cheerful. Took to Nita the towel I embroidered for her. Packed further.

June 2, Wed. Riola planned a "surprise (?) party" for me at her home tonight, my children and some teachers.

June 3, Thurs. Worked on reports etc. Went to pieces, and so cut two parties. Spent the evening in Mary's room. I am grateful for Minna.

June 4, Fri. Felt perhaps I could endure the unendurable. Heard from Mrs. Hurst again, and two letters from Alice. My children were dear when they came for their cards. Final packing, etc. Not quite so worn.

June 5, Sat. Train. Farewells to Williams. The children blest me. Sugar with me to Needles. Have written to Alice in my berth. I cannot say what I feel. I shall try to live truly

LOS ANGELES

Jun. 6, Sun. Alhambra, reached here about seven, and all day long I have watched Dorothy, my own little niece. I have held her close, and tried to see life aright. I have loved too much. Alice and Ernest are good for me, too, and a joy

June 7, Mon. Reveled in Dorothy, took her out in her carriage, lay by her resting for hours. Talked much with Alice.

June 8, Tues. After another night of wonderful sleep. I think wee Dorothy has saved me! I am trying to see the sunshine of life. Played Five Hundred.

June 9, Wed. Went to Los Angeles, and tried to forget it was Ruth's city. Enjoyed the partial care of Dorothy, and buying baby things.

June 10, Thurs. Picked berries and cleaned house for Alice, and did other work that I enjoyed. I feel nearer serenity through Dorothy

June 11, Fri. It is such a joy to help take care of my "baby!" I feel she belongs to me, too. I try to see God's purposes.

June 12, Sat. Tried to help Alice sew, I enjoy her very much, and Dorothy is an unutterable blessing.

June 13, Sun. Kept care of the baby while Alice and Ernest went to church. Just before dusk came to Pasadena to Mamie's.

CLAREMONT, POMONA COLLEGE

June 14, Mon. Claremont. Last night Mamie blest me most deeply, I talked to her for hours. Helen did not get on at Glendora. Need she suffer, too? Juliet took charge of me. Went with May and Roland to class of 1911 party.

June 15, Tues. I truly enjoyed deeply Class Day, all the reunions. Dr. Parker and Deak took me out in machines. Called on Alice Stearns and Charlotte. Dinner at Maynard's. With the Roofs to the play about Hopi Indians.

June 16, Wed. Helen with me at Summer Hall. Commencement splendid. Went to Music Hall with Helen. To the fine banquet with Deak.

June 17, Thurs. Glendora. Visited the Maynard's with Helen, then went home with her. Long visits in the afternoon and at night that were a great blessing. I enjoyed her brother.

June 18, Fri. Claremont. Again with Edna for the night, as a year ago today! Supper here then to Gertrude Bacon's wedding. I am glad I am here.

June 19, Sat. Alhambra. Gladys Somers called before Edna and I were up. We slept late after talking long the night before. She is wonderful, and I feel much better. Had a good call on the Wingards, and then gladly came back to Alice and her family.

ELSINORE

June 21, Mon. Came with Alice and the baby, Ernest, came at night. Oh so good to be home, and with my dear family!

June 22, Tues. Did some household work, and unpacked my trunk, getting my room in order. Enjoyed having all the family together. D. is adored.

June 23, Wed. Talked and wrote some letters, one to a strange man in Phoenix.[33] Worked a little. Tired, but not unserene.

June 24, Thurs. Alice and her family left to pack their things. It seems too good to be true that they are to stay here! To watch Dorothy all summer! Studied some Algebra.

June 25, Fri. Still resting and writing letters, and studying, I like this place. Helped with the "wash." Mother and I drove to town at dusk, and talked.

June 27, Sun. Lovely "family" day. Dorothy is so bewitching! Wrote cards and notes to some of my schoolchildren and to others.

June 30, Wed. Went to the village and met Minna at noon. It is good to have her. My family are so lovely! Ernest sang for us.

July 2, Fri. Helped with a washing and caring for chickens. Finished writing to my Williams children. Adored Dorothy, Alice, and Ernest. Minna and I walked to the Matilija poppy fields.

July 3, Sat. Another busy day. Minna and I went to the village with the old horse, and called on Pat.

July 6, Tues. Studied Geometry, rested, fed chickens, wrote cards, etc.

July 8, Thurs. Studied. Aunt Mamie and Minna and I talked and looked over old things upstairs. Cooked a little. Burned a bundle of letters.

July 10, Sat. Tried to gird up my soul and body after a night of bad dreams. Climbed with Minna.

July 11, Sun. Felt better in all ways. Read, cooked a little, rested and wrote letters, and walked and talked with the family and Minna.

July 13, Tues. Wrote to Floss that I wouldn't be at her house party. Ironed and sewed. Held Dorothy at my side on a bed under the trees again. Walked.

July 14, Wed. We went after wood in gypsy fashion. After an early waffle supper, Father, Mother, Aunt Mamie, Minna and I climbed our fine hill again.

---

33 Elsie corresponded with a Mr. Craig who was involved with Karl's hospitalization. He apparently reported to her on Karl's progress.

July 15, Thurs. Packed my suitcase. Had a much appreciated letter from Mr. Craig, and sat up late to answer it. How much I feel!

LOS ANGELES

July 16, Fri. Glendora. Minna and I left before seven. Errands in Los Angeles. Helen's for overnight.

July 17, Sat. Pasadena. Rose at five, and went through lovely lifting fog to see Minna off from L.A. at 7:25. Shopped, and then came here and called on the Hands. At Mamie's now. I am rich in friends.

SAN DIEGO

July 18, Sun. Balboa. Mamie helped very much, and I decided to send my letter if Alice approves. Leisurely good day at the Hands'. Met Helen and came here.

July 19, Mon. Helen and her grandmother and I sat on the sand. Read aloud senior play The Gods are Good.

July 20, Tues. Had a fine time in the surf with Helen. Gay family "party" on the mainland. The brother, with all his degrees, is truly interesting. Helen and I talk at night.

July 22, Thurs. Helen and I went for cockles and got them on mud flats. Fun. Read from book of sermons The Test. Read Arnold over the water. Phosphorescence and moonlight over the ocean. It has helped us both to be together.

LOS ANGELES

July 23, Fri. Left Helen and met Ivy We both went to Ruth's home and stayed overnight. How my throat has ached with unshed tears! But even this helps, and Ivy makes it easier.

July 24, Sat. Long Beach, talked until afternoon, when Ivy and I left and came to her home here. "I only am left" of the Triumvirate, but God is good and it must be best. Love lives.

July 26, Mon. Elsinore, I had lunch in Claremont at the Maynard's and a rich few minutes with Edna. Ernest met me. It is good to be home.

July 28, Wed. Feel much more rested, and I appreciate the change. Aunt Mamie and I canned 33 pints of peaches and berries.

July 29, Thurs. Still feeling better. Began Tennyson's <u>Princess</u> and studied algebra and sewed. It is good to be with my dear family

July 31, Sat. Spent many hours sorting letters and souvenirs, and then made a great fire of almost all of them. I have relived my life. I must begin again.

Aug. 1, Sun. Went with the family to church. Reveled in Dorothy, and read much of Scott's <u>Rob Roy</u>

Aug. 3, Tues. HOT. Washed clothes, cleaned with gasoline; lived on ice cream.

Aug. 6, Fri. I'll try to be more self reliant and "fit" in every way than I was a year ago, or yesterday! Studied Emerson's <u>Compensation</u>. Another letter from Mr. Craig. I am glad of good news, but must be brave in hearing the finality for myself! [Mr. Craig may have advised Elsie not to consider marriage to Karl as an option.]

Aug. 7, Sat. Weather still bad. More serene today

Aug. 8, Sun. I remember a year ago today Family prayers and a family day Sorry Hylinda and I have such a different religious viewpoint. Worked on Kodak book, putting in Cornville pictures. Rested.

SAN DIEGO

Aug. 10, Tues. A year ago I saw Ruthie for the last time. At 7:15 left by auto with Father, Mother, Alice, Ernest, and baby Lovely machine trip by coast route to San Diego.

Aug. 11, Wed. Saw Alice Parker and rested my soul. With her met the family and spent the rest of the day at Exposition. Wonderful grounds, band concert and great organ.[34]

---

34 From "Exposition Beautiful, Opens Gates to World," by D. C. Collier: "Pluck and perseverance have triumphed. The Panama-California Exposition in San Diego is a reality. San Diego now presents to the world such an Exposition as never before was built. The claim of those who originated it, that it would be unique and that it would have a charm and present an atmosphere never before attained by any exposition has been fully carried out" (*San Diego Union*, January 1, Special Section, II, 2:1–4).

August 12, Thurs. A restful day. Rose late, and walked through Balboa Park to see Alice. Went to her room. Read <u>American Literature</u> in afternoon. Rowing in a barge.

Aug. 14, Sat. Coronado. Alice and I began living in Tent City together. [It was popular to vacation in tents along the beach at Coronado Island.] How good to be with her! Heard the concert and talked.

Aug. 15, Sun. After talking all night, truly rested in the day. On the beach Alice read aloud to me, Mary R. S. Andrews' <u>Courage of the Commonplace</u>.

Aug. 16, Mon. Elsinore. After a peaceful night of deep rest and all the tonic air of every kind, chiefly Alice's, I have indeed a wonderful "fresh grip." I am glad to be home, too.

Aug. 19, Thurs. A more horribly hot day than the last. I packed more or less all day. My family helped beautifully.

Aug. 20, Fri. My last day at home, everybody helping with my things. I hate to leave! Held Dorothy and talked with Hylinda.

Aug. 21, Sat. Long Beach. Said goodbye to Hylinda and Aunt Mamie, though that hurt. Came with the rest of the family, a beautiful auto trip, to Long Beach.

Aug. 24, Tues. Woke sad, but steadied myself somewhat. Worked a little.

Aug. 25, Wed. Dentist and shopping and lunch downtown with Father and Mother. Went to the Harnetts'. I feel much.

Aug. 26, Thurs. Train. Went by auto with the family to city. A lovely time. Mother and Father saw me off. I hated to go!

Aug. 27, Fri. Williams. Enjoyed the party of Texas teachers on board. Met by Mr. Gold. Good to be with Minna. Saw supt. and talked over the work. I'm glad I shall need to work so hard. Did some "settling" in our little house, and studied.

Aug. 28, Sat. Teachers meeting. Worked hard over plans. Delighted to have work I want, almost all English. We finished getting our house in order.

Aug. 29, Sun. Wrote home and to Alice in detail about the English work. Mildred Murphy, Pomona College (1914), came to teach, and I tried to make her feel at home. She is dear.

Elsie with her Williams students

Aug. 30, Mon. School, though not regular work. I have ten classes, 3 H. S. English, and grade Grammar and Reading and Spelling in 7th and 8th, and 7th Geography. Enthusiastic over work and glad to see children. [The *Williams News* mentions school opening with 220 pupils in contrast to the small Cornville school.]

Aug. 31, Tues. First day of regular school. Busy, but glad indeed of that and my special work I've always wanted. Downtown with Georgia. Read Myths to Minna.

Sept. 1, Wed. Enjoyed my work, especially the Myth talk to English I. Read English and American History of Lit. in evening; and a story from the Alhambra aloud.

Sept. 2, Thurs. Composition Day at school. Worked afterward, as usual, and then ordered groceries with Minna.

Sept 3, Fri. Rain part of day. Wish I could forget the memories this weekend brings. School helps. Today with Mildred Murphy, Miss Watson and Philip, Minna and I called on Miss Chapman and at the Gold's.

Sept. 4, Sat. Why write of our day of household work? Yet I enjoyed it, and made myself enjoy our various chats on the street this evening.

Sep. 5, Sun. Took Miss Chapman to church. The communion service blessed me. A group of us walked on the ridge. I wrote letters at night. I try . . .

Sept 6, Mon. A very busy day at school, and a busy evening over schoolwork. I am grateful for work, and work worth doing.

Sept. 7, Tues. Another day of hard work, prepared questions on Irving's life, etc. Callers.

Sept. 8, Wed. A Miss Davis of Boston visited English III, and pleased me. We took her to the picnic by the lake, large, bright affair. Poems about teachers read, teachers hilarious afterward.

Sept. 9, Thurs. Letter from Phoenix again, relieving me further. But still I ache with keen sympathy, as well as for myself. Work and callers.

Sept. 10, Fri. Went to a dance, I did not fully appreciate, with Mr. Latham, Mr. Twitty (driving) and four other teachers.

Sept. 11, Sat. Minna and Miss Watson came. Cleaned house, did errands, wrote letters. Read <u>Ancient Mariner</u> to Minna.

Sep. 12, Sun. Took Mildred to church, then called on her, and Miss Mitchell and Miss More and Mary. Rested and read English work.

Sept. 13, Mon. So busy at school that the hours there fly by, and the work is delight. Usual Monday teacher's meeting.

Sept. 15, Wed. Trying to adapt myself to new geography arrangements. Georgia and Miss Watson came to an informal supper, which we all enjoyed.

Sept. 16, Thurs. Hurt my neck, and so had a trying day. Not able to look on all sides as a teacher should! Letters that made me think.

Sept. 17, Fri. Worked late at school, despite my neck.

Sept. 18, Sat. My neck is better, but kept from The Three Sisters tramp. Enjoyed quiet day alone because I accomplished so many pieces of school work, making out questions, planning, etc.

Sep. 19, Sun. What have I done or gained in the past year? I shall try to make the new one count. Took Miss Laney to church. Made calls, had Miss Chapman, and Phillip for tea.

Sept. 20, Mon. Usual long teachers meeting. Finished Scott's fascinating <u>Talisman</u> at night.

Sept. 21, Tues. Outlined <u>The Talisman</u>, I do enjoy the English work, and am glad to be too busy. Tonight I pray it may be a friend's last in bondage. [Karl?]

Sept. 22, Wed. Another full day. Worked as usual in my room after school. Sugar, Lou, and Alice Barclay had supper with us. Minna talked with me, and we walked. Reread <u>Vicar of Wakefield</u>.

Sept. 23, Thurs. Again preparing for exams, with a vengeance, copying questions for individual pupils. Voyt Miller took us for an auto ride on Grand Canyon Road.

Sept. 25, Sat. A day of varied work and some rest. Martha Stanley and Miss Laney came to luncheon, so we cooked a little. We shopped by mail.

Sept. 26, Sun. Philip Chapman spent the day with us. We called on the Peets and Mrs. Nordyke. Had dinner at the Sine's!

Sept. 27, Mon. Still correcting papers. Teachers meeting. Went with Miss Watson to call on Riola, who is ill.

Sept. 28, Tues. Visitors Day at school. I enjoyed praise! Educational meeting of Women's Club and teachers at four.

Letter from Elsie's father
Elsinore, Sept. 28, 1915

Dear Elsie,

   I have enjoyed having your good letter, and am very pleased that you are feeling so well, and like your work and surroundings so much. I think you are very fortunate in having such a nice girl as Minna to live with. We are all well except Aunt Mamie, she is better but does not improve as we would like to have her. We are afraid the doctor gives her too many drugs.

We miss you very much,
Love, Father

Sept. 29, Wed. School out at 11:30, we took 8 little Mexicans into Barnes' Circus and so had a good afternoon. Skimmed Bret Harte's <u>Waif of the Plains</u>. Letter from Mrs. Hurst relieved me in several ways. Walked to dam.

Sept. 30, Thurs. Worked on report cards and corrected themes as today's extra work. Also, made out questions for the <u>Odyssey</u>.

Oct. 1, Fri. Such a full day! Went for mail before school, hoping to hear better news of Aunt Mamie. Went to see if Senaida Valdez couldn't be kept in school. Went on errands in evening with Minna, and called on Minnie D., with letter of introduction to Alice M. Parker.

Oct. 2, Sat. Washed and ironed. Lu and Sugar called, and Philip. Mr. Polson asked us to go by auto to the Canyon if his cousin came early in the morning.

Oct. 3, Sun. Rose early and wrote letters while waiting to see if we were going to Grand Canyon. Cousin, Miss Collins came at noon. Dinner at Polsons' and ride to K.Y. ranch. On way to Flying H a mishap, and we three girls waited in the wilds 4 hours! Erle brought us back after we were rescued at 9:20. Supper at Polsons'.

Oct. 4, Mon. Busy day at school. Took Miss Collins downtown. Miss C. is charming. Minna and I asked the girls for supper by the lake to meet her. Gay time.

Oct. 5, Tues. Women's Club at Mrs. Robinson's. Pioneer tales told by pioneers themselves.[35] Very interesting. Mrs. Gold and Myra and the girls of her house called. I'm too tired. Read after I got into bed, <u>Vanity Fair</u>.

Oct. 6, Wed. Miss Collins visited English III. I received 6 letters. Trimmed my new hat and my old one. We went to the depot with Miss C. Now I'm going to <u>Vanity Fair</u> again.

Oct. 7, Thurs. Called on Mrs. Dye, and left cards for Mrs. Boone and Mrs. Pierce, not home, went to Miss Chapman's for dinner. Finished reading <u>Vanity Fair</u>; read first to Caroline.

---

35 Elsie recalled the story an old woman had told that day. Her husband had been a cavalry officer in Arizona during the days of Indian raids. He was to meet another group, but when he arrived all had been killed; the covered wagons were still smoldering.

Oct. 8, Fri. Outlined <u>Vanity Fair</u>; and began Kipling's <u>Kim</u>, never read before. Called on the Sines. Went with Jerry Duffield to get my freight, box of books. Books are good!

Oct. 9, Sat. Cleaned part of house and yard. Finished <u>Kim</u>, delightful. Made out questions on it, and read parts again to Minna. P.S. On this date Jack Roberts started to work in Williams.

Oct. 10, Sun. Went to church, helped by a fine sermon by Mr. Boone. Rested, and went with Grace Sine to hear a good Y.M.C.A. worker from Ceylon.

Oct. 11, Mon. Worked at school until five; Martha Stanley for supper; read almost all of Kipling's <u>Plain Tales from the Hills</u>. They do not mean nearly as much to me as <u>Kim</u>.

Oct. 12, Tues. Women's Club at Mrs. Cureton's. Mrs. A. Miller brought me back by machine, and then Grace and I walked downtown. Made out H. S. examinations.

Oct. 13, Wed. Meeting after school to plan further for Card Club. I am disgusted, don't want to spend so much time that way, or leave Minna. Wrote notes and school reports.

Oct. 14, Thurs. Several letters from Cornville did me good. Went to a card party at Edna Buglen's with Mr. Kimball! Dancing afterward. Enjoyed it.

Oct. 15, Fri. Today was "the morning after the night before!" The usual Friday rush. Some of the children came for help to the house. Read aloud from <u>Atlantic Monthly</u>.

Oct. 16, Sat. Slept late and felt better. A beautiful day. Did much work (even piling some wood!) and tramped on the ridge with M. and Miss Watson.

Oct. 17, Sun. Took Mildred to church. Wrote some letters and did some Christmas planning. Miss. W., Minna, Philip, Grace, M. and I took our supper to the ridge. Beautiful!

Oct. 18, Mon. After all, we are not going to Institute!

Oct. 19, Tues. Minnie D. seems more devoted than ever, though I was afraid I had been too severe Friday about her glasses. Wrote to say Phoenix will not materialize! I am more relieved, but ache. [If Else had gone to Institute in Phoenix, she surely would have seen Karl.]

Oct. 20, Wed. Beautiful autumn day! Very busy. Piled wood. Grace called. Had a letter from Marguerite. Indeed I must trust. My problems are settled for me.

Oct. 21, Thurs. Accomplished a great deal of work at school. Supper on hill near the Sines', chiefly teachers. Then Miss W. came home with us. Fudge and discussions.

Oct. 22, Fri. Flagstaff. Exams at school. Came home and made ready for "Flag." Nita and Ferd met us, Sugar and Minna and I, at 8:15. Mrs. Barney was with us on the train. We "visited" in the evening.

Oct 23, Sat. Long day, with wonderful beauty and yet much heartache. This town gives thoughts. [This was where Karl planned to eventually have his own ranch.] We went in the "Hup" [Hupmobile] over 100 miles, through pines, cedars, and desert. Visited Indian ruins and saw round-up of 2,000 head; lunch on brink of Canyon Diablo. Volcanic and meteor peaks, and wind-swept rocks, the cottonwoods gold, on Little Colorado. Bought rug at Tolchaco trading post. Sunset across painted desert. Full moon and pines.

Oct. 24, Sun. Williams. Rose late. Talking and callers. Went to Fort Valley, 10 miles out, where Ferd had been dipping sheep. Skimmed Zane Gray's Light of Western Stars and Arma K. Green's Amethyst Box as a diversion at lightning pace. Train late. Got home at 11:30. Nita is dear, and the trip helped with inspiration and a fresh grip.

Oct. 25, Mon. Busy and weary. Correcting exam papers. Railed again at the triviality of Williams, and then resolved afresh to try to improve my attitude.

Oct. 26, Tues. Corrected more papers. Called on Mrs. Winans. Planned much of work of next month for English classes, and enjoyed it.

Oct. 27, Wed. Pretended room was Olympus in English I. Corrected papers, and wrote a long letter home. Mrs. Sine and Grace, Miss W., Mildred, Minna and I had supper on the hill, grand view. I resolve more firmly to be cheerful.

Oct. 28, Thurs. Struggles, partly amusing, with discipline. Went to a league Halloween party and came home early with Minnie. Added later, here first (to my recollection) saw John John Planwydd Roberts, though did not meet him until Jan. 8.

Letter from Dale Girdner
Cornville, Az.
Oct 28, 1915

Dear Teacher,

I received your letter of the 18th last Friday and have read it at least as much as a dozen times. I was certainly glad to hear from you again. Say talking about cranky teachers they've shure got a cranky one this year. I'm sure nobody could call you a cranky teacher. There has been three deaths on the creek since I wrote to you last. Mr. Topping and Mr. Donaldson and another man you didn't know. There was this mix-up at the Hurst's the other day Ramon and another feller got into it about a horse. Ramon threatened to kill the other feller. A few days after Ramon was sitting down fixing his harness with his revolver by his side and the other feller come along with his six shooter in his pocket and his hand on it. Ramon reached for his gun and the other feller shot him and just took a little hide off of his shoulder. Ramon dropped his gun and the other feller popped him one right in the top of his head and killed him. The next day they buried him on top of the hill. Tuce Reese preached the funeral and Dick Duncan was undertaker. Well guess your tired of reading this kind of dope so I'll change the subject for awhile. Gene Lee is getting lots of experience riding now. He bought him a horse on the Verde and it threw him four times but he's got so he can ride him now. He says it's the buckinest horse he ever seen or rode. I'm going to start to school in about 3 weeks now if I can. You said you expected great things from us three kids. Do you think I'm going to be some great orator or a New York lawyer going struttin around with a high top collar and a diamond ring on my finger? Not me that fits Stanleys case better'n mine. No you have a better opinion of me than I have of myself. This isn't as good a place to work as

Wincoop's was. No, I don't boss the Indians around. Most everybody tries to boss me. I only get to boss one Mexican irrigator nobody can talk to him but me, and I do a bum job at it. Then there's one little papoose I get to paddle once in a while and make it holler when the old squaw ain't lookin. I don't get to ride much. She has about 80 head of cattle I get to look after and go to the post office once in awhile and ride home Saturday nights. Well it is nearly 11 o'clock and I was at a party at Wincoop's last night and didn't get in til 2 o'clock and at literary the night before til midnight so will close for tonight.

> As Ever,
> Dale Girdner

Oct. 29, Fri. All kinds of work at school made my day even fuller than usual. Cleaned house and did some more washing. Miss Watson and M. Stanley spent the evening.

Oct. 30, Sat. A wonderful day. Grace, Miss C, Philip, M. and I tramped 12 or 15 miles, climbing Bill Williams. I saw Mingus Mtn. again, in a glorious view of crests and peaks. I feel stronger and more cheerful. I felt so well that I worked hard afterward.

Oct. 31, Sun. Heard a wonderful sermon by Mr. Boone on Immortality. We got our own noon meal. Miss Watson and her mother called on us. Wrote letters. Went to the Sweetwoods' for dinner in honor of M's birthday. Went to League. Wrote letters. Later: In the cake drew the prophetic ring! True Halloween.

Nov. 1, Mon. Up too late last night! We went with Mrs. and Miss Watson to Miss Chapman's and sewed. I began the pillow slips for Minna.

Nov. 2, Tues. We had Martha Stanley for a birthday supper, with candles, cake, etc. Darned hose and read in Franklin's <u>Autobiography</u>.

Nov. 3, Wed. Washed and ironed some clothes after school. Wrote some cards and notes; some to people ill or deserving congratulations. Read good magazines.

Nov. 4, Thurs. Planned work ahead. Read in <u>Autobiography</u>. My blistered foot from the Bill Williams tramp is annoying. But I must not worry!

Nov. 5, Fri. Pinepark. After school went with Minna to the Parker's ranch, seven and a half miles from town. Drove out with Max and Ella Parker. Saw a wonderful sunset on the way. Began re-reading <u>Silas Marner</u>.

Nov. 6, Sat. A rainy day. Worked on pillowslips for Minna. Mrs. Parker told us so much about railroading we feel acquainted with it!

Nov. 7, Sun. Williams. Drove back during the afternoon, after a restful morning at the ranch. More interesting conversation. Mrs. Parker did me good by her cheer.

Nov. 8, Mon. Finished Franklin's <u>Autobiography</u> and <u>Silas Marner</u>.

Nov. 9, Tues. Rain. Went to Women's Club, where M. Gorky's <u>Lower Depths</u> was discussed. Mr. Boone called. Miss Chapman and Philip came to supper.

Nov. 10, Wed. Remembering a year ago. Snow. Got our own lunch again and found Mrs. Hays cannot board us after this. Reading <u>David Copperfield</u>.

Nov. 11, Thurs. Mrs. Hughes was our hostess for luncheon at Mr. Hess, and again for sandwiches after school! Trying to keep warm. Remember a couplet of Rossetti's.[36]

Nov. 12, Fri. Luncheon again at Mr. Hess! Busy day, as usual. Cleaned house after school. Read in <u>David Copperfield</u>.

Nov. 13, Sat. Washed, including blankets, and ironed. Corrected papers. Minnie brought us candy. Mrs. Plummer called. Maladjustments. I must go on.

Nov. 14, Sun. The Golds'. Again I make special resolves and try to start anew. It is a year since I have seen, and I ought to find again much in life.

Nov. 15, Mon. Called on Mary, who has sprained her ankle; Velma, who is sick; and Vivi, who wanted me to see the new baby sister. Read Holmes' <u>Guardian Angel</u> in evening, which I've read before. Appreciated it more.

---

36 Dante Rossetti wrote poems dealing with romance and lost loves. In "Lost Days" he spoke of those days as "golden coins squandered and still to pay."

Nov.16, Tues. Discussed school plans with Supt., and called on Nita. Wrote to Helen and mid-week card home, and corrected long reports.

Nov. 17, Wed. Objected to helping Georgia with the library, Mr. Latham asked me! Asked by Mrs. Reese for supper. Sewed there. Read in <u>Les Miserables</u> later.

Nov. 18, Thurs. Compliments from Mr. Latham, Supt., did me good. Called on the Boones and Mildred Murphy, and went with her to ask about trains home for Christmas, five weeks!

Nov. 19, Fri. Monthly examinations. Corrected many of the papers, and went to bed almost ill from overwork.

Nov. 20, Sat. Still Williams. Rose late, from need, but corrected more papers. Called on Lois, who has a hurt ankle. Wrote Christmas cards. Rested.

Nov. 21, Sun. Memories still! Went to church. We took Rose to dinner, and then made a call. Riola talked with me later while I rested, almost ill.

Nov. 22, Mon. Busy day, working on grades, report cards, etc. Called on Mrs. Gold, and stopped at the Boone's again, this time for S. S. material. Feel better.

Nov. 23, Tues. Amusing round with Kenneth R. at school, not wholly amusing either; but it turned out well. Carried in wood, etc.

Nov. 24, Wed. Box from home. After school washed clothes and also engaged a new Mexican washwoman. Read to Minna from <u>Bleak House</u>. Remembered other Thanksgiving Eves, and Triumvirate.

Nov. 25, Thurs. Thanksgiving Day. Had a pleasant dinner at the Udin's. Stopped at the Gold's, with plans for Canyon trip. Prepared for it. Light supper at the Sweetwoods'! I am thankful for much.

9

A Year Is a Long Time

"I constantly make new resolves. A Year is a long time. I must push on."

Elsie confided to her diary that she was trying to see life "aright." She also revealed, "I have loved too much." Returning home a week after the tragic news about Karl, Elsie draws from her family's love. But having burned Karl's letters does not seem to erase her thoughts of him. Throughout the fall months she wrote of haunting memories. Yet she also wrote that through it all she was trying to see God's purpose. Ultimately, she appeared to accept the finality of a lost relationship with Karl. As she moved on, she found diversion through reading books and teaching, as the activities in Williams, the card parties and the movies, suddenly all seemed so trivial to her.

Nov. 26, 1915, Fri. Bass Camp, Grand Canyon. Mr. and Mrs. Gold, baby Myra, Minna and I left Williams by auto, and came 90 miles. Ran into trees and a bank! Beautiful trip. Saw Canyon at dusk. Lost the road, ran on rock and camped, sleeping on buckbrush boughs. Rescued after midnight, and drive to Bass Camp. Saw Canyon by moonlight. Wonderful!

Nov. 27, Sat. El Tovar Settlement, Grand Canyon. Mr. Bass took Minna and me down trail as far as cliff dwellings, 500 feet below rim. Explained fossils, formations, etc. in fascinating way. Back 24 miles to El Tovar village. All night at Mr. Bass' headquarters.[37] Last of five "river scouts" came in while we were there, after 45 hours without food. We were to have met them at foot of trail for movies; but they were wrecked. Fascinating local color.

Nov. 28, Sun. Williams. Minna and I walked to rim and along it. Met Miss C. and P. at Lookout, and took them back to be introduced to Mr. Bass. Came the 66 miles home. Tired but blest. Grace and Mrs. Whiting. Wrote Christmas cards.

Nov. 29, Mon. Ruth's birthday. I remember her, but am uplifted. I dream of her. Callers. Read <u>Bleak House</u>.

---

37 Among Elsie's papers was a pamphlet by W. W. Bass, "Rhymes and Jingles." It is autographed by the author. His business card reads, "Poet and Geologist of the Grand Canyon. Rhymes and Jingles By W. W. Bass, The Grand Canyon Guide. Copyrighted 1909 W. W. Bass. J. F. Rowny Press, Los Angeles 1915."

Stranded at the edge of the Grand Canyon

Nov. 30, Tues. Supper on the hill. Lost in <u>Bleak House</u>. Read it until midnight. Wish I were more like Esther Summerson [heroine of *Bleak House*].

Dec. 1, Wed. Wrote to Alice M. Parker about Canyon, and account of trip for <u>Williams News</u>. Warmer than usual, tho Dec. 1.

Dec. 1, 1915

Dear Alice,

Your card came today, and I rejoice to think you are in the mountains. I keep remembering it with pleasure and hopefulness. I feel you will soon feel much, much, stronger in the mountain air. How I hope that will soon prove true.

We had a wonderful time at the canyon, and unique experiences. We left here Friday between nine and ten; Mr. and Mrs. Gold and adorable little Myra, aged 18 months, in front, and we behind with groceries and a suitcase, etc. We had our foot warmers and our muffs, heavy gloves, close outing caps, and sweaters under our coats. The morning was clear and cold, and the stinging air was a joy as we spun along. The day's journey was to be about ninety miles, as it is 66 to the canyon settlement, Hotel El Tovar, etc., and Mr. Bass' camp is 24 miles beyond that.

Mr. Gold is Mr. Bass' attorney, and a humorous, kindly man we have always enjoyed. Mrs. Gold is a tonic. Mr. Bass is, as he says, "poet and geologist of the Grand Canyon." He has lived in this region since the beginnings and at the canyon for thirty years. He came here when he had been proclaimed an incurable in the East, upsetting the doctor's verdicts by living in a cave near Williams. It was a tiny village about then, with thirty saloons, most of them in tents. When the railroad first came, tourists at the station could hear the town as it was being "shot up." An enemy sent seventeen Indians after Mr. Bass when he had come into Williams to vote one day. So you see he is really a pioneer.

Mr. Bass owns various houses at different points along the canyon, and a trail that includes a ferry over the Colorado River in the depths of the Canyon. He has automobiles, carriages, and saddle horses to take tourists about, but the railroad is his mortal foe, (and tries to keep the tourists ignorant of him). Only the other day, Mr. Gold had to make a flying trip to El Tovar to represent one of Mr. Bass' drivers. A certain Bert Louzon had been having a fight with a Santa Fe policeman because he had dared to speak to a tourist and was accused of having solicited her patronage. Nevertheless, great scientists seek for Mr. Bass and take long trips with him over his beloved trails. He is a scientist himself. Mr. Bass rather expects to go on a lecture tour soon and wanted moving pictures of the canyon as illustrations. A trio of "river scouts," led by a Mr. Russel, began to take pictures for the "movies" the other day, shooting the rapid of the Colorado River in boats built for such purposes. Of course they, like others who have gone thru the canyon, were taking their lives in their hands. Mr. Bass told Mr. Gold if he would bring some women to his camp, to have their pictures taken on his trail to prove women can go down it, he (Mr. Bass) would take them across the ferry at the foot of the trail, etc. His words were, "You furnish the ladies, and I'll furnish the eats." At least, so Mr. Gold tells it. We were asked to be the ladies![38]

The country between here and El Tovar is wild and fascinating; desert and cedars and pines are there, according to the altitude. We were glad to go by machine. Mr. Gold has only had the car a short time, and is a novice. We ran into several trees and a steep bank en route, but otherwise got along splendidly! We had a fleeting glimpse of

The girls were supposed to ride in this cage across the Canyon while being filmed.

the Canyon at El Tovar, some miles beyond our picnic luncheon, and then we struck inward again for the cut across to Bass camp. We went thru the wildest narrow canyon I ever dreamed of. I wonder if Kubla Khan isn't like that! We went thru lovely meadow glades in the cedar and piñon forest, with far views of the Peaks and Bill Williams and a few other blue wonders. Sometimes we had sight of the opposite rim of the Grand Canyon, 2000 feet higher than this side.

When it grew dark we began to watch more closely for the fresh wagon tracks we were to follow. Mr. Bass had preceded us with saddle horses, food, etc., and we constantly expected to overtake him. Suddenly in deep twilight, after a radiant sunset, we found ourselves on the very edge of the Canyon. To come upon the vastness abruptly at that hour was marvelous!

---

38 W. W. Bass wrote, "At the foot of the Bass Trail is the only ferry and cable crossing in the Grand Canyon where men and animals can be transported from one side of the river to the other" ("Rhymes and Jingles by W. W. Bass").

To make a long story short, we took the wrong road, which was full of brush, stones and stumps. Even after our lights finally worked it was awful. At every turn we rushed upon, I wondered if it would bring us again to the Brink. I shouldn't have been at all surprised if we had suddenly gone over. At last we crashed upon such a huge rock that the machine stuck. Meanwhile we had all decided (except Myra) that we must have gone at least 10 miles beyond the camp, in some way. Something was broken; and as we were in utterly unknown country, and even if we were near the camp, twenty miles from any other habitation, we decided that we would have to camp. If we had passed the camp the only thing ahead, so far as we knew, was the Havasupi Indian village, many, many, miles beyond. After that, somewhere across the desert, California. We could not tell whether we were a few feet or a few miles from the rim.

We built a fire, and then gathered buckbrush for a bed. There were two quilts. One was to go under us. Only one was over us, five of us, tho it was so cold that the water in the water bag soon froze solid. We piled a screen of piñon branches at our heads, and lay down in the road. First there was Mr. Gold, with his gun and rifle, and Myra on an auto cushion. Then Mrs.Gold, and we girls. At one of Mr. Bass' houses, where we had stopped for water, at the settlement, Bert Louzon (with his face still showing the policeman's fury) had given us an extra foot warmer. We had them all hot, at our feet. Minna and I slept on our Muffs. We gave Mrs. Gold the Pomona pillow I had tucked in to keep us from too much sliding on the back seat. The felt cover we took off, as an extra cover for Myra. The fire died down, and the world was very still. We were beyond even the range cattle. Once the wind stirred the piñon trees near us, and its chill went to our bones.

I had really slept, at last, when suddenly I heard Mrs. Gold saying in a stage whisper, "Frank! I hear a horse!" Sure enough, we heard one, far off; and the moon had come up. I thot it was almost dawn. Mr. Gold took his gun and rose. It was another of Mr. Bass' drivers, who was galloping 24 miles at night to call off the trip down the trail next day. The river scouts had been wrecked before getting as far down the Colorado as that (they had started from Bright Angel trail, from El Tovar). Two had just staggered into Mr. Bass' house at the settlement, white, the driver said, as ghosts. They had somehow, without food or water, climbed out of the Canyon without a trail. It is inspiring to think how people can perform the Impossible! But they had somehow lost Russel in the depths. It was terrible to think of him on this icy night, down there somewhere, with the vast heights above, and no food or water. The apparatus was in the lost boat with everything else. [The "apparatus," the movie camera, would have been a very expensive piece of equipment.]

After our thrills over this tale, the rider informed us he would go on to Bass Camp and bring back a wagon for us. Mrs. Gold said that would hardly be worth his trouble, and then we learned we were only a mile and a half from the camp, and that it was not yet midnight! We girls lay there and giggled like schoolgirls.

So at one fifteen or so, Mr. Bass was warmly greeting us and showing us our rooms. The house had been vacant all summer. Cowboys sometimes stopped for a night. The sheets last used (and how long used?) were on our beds. The comforts weren't perfumed! Mr. Bass is a gentleman, but his wife and children are in California for educational purposes, and I suppose a man adapts himself to a cattle country. Mr. Gold informed his wife we ought to be grateful for sheets at all. I put a riding skirt over my pillow and slept between comforts in preference. It was all a part of the experience.

The next morning while we dressed we saw from the windows the rosy light brightening over the Canyon. We were on the very rim. I wish you had seen it. The driver helped Mr. Bass get breakfast. There were cobwebs in the edge of the frying pan while the pancakes cooked, but I never was so glad for thick coffee or any other kind, before. Minna and I cleaned the kitchen while we washed the dishes.

Altho the trip down to the river was abandoned, Mr. Bass wanted to take us girls 500 feet down (that many feet straight down, a good walk by trail) as far as some Indian ruins. Of course we went. They were interesting caves, with tree trunks in them cut with stone hatchets 2,000 years ago, I believe our guide said! He showed us the secret cisterns he had discovered down there. To look up and on and down from the side of that endless, stupendous cliff was unutterable. And oh the colorings in sunlight and shadow! I dug in one cave and ate piñon nuts like an old squaw, and meditated. Everywhere the ruined Indian fort by the camp seemed to be watching us. It had suggested to Mr. Bass where the trail should be built.

Meanwhile we absorbed information by the ream. The fossils at our feet, the minerals, the jogs in the rock layers, the immensity, everything was made the illustration of a lecture. I felt as ignorant as an insect, or more so. Anecdotes of the world famed scientists who have been there with him, jokes of every kind, reflections on philosophy and God: these added to the interest of the theme. We were entranced. I don't know a thing about geology, and there was the world's best object museum for that subject. I still feel so insignificant that I haven't the audacity to feel my sorrows as deeply as I did before. I mean that very seriously.

On our return we found that the machine had been overhauled and brought to camp by Mr. Gold. The wit Mr. Gold and Mr. Bass threw at each other enlivened our meals. After luncheon we started back for El Tovar, since we might as well, and Myra wasn't very trim. ["Proper" Elsie would not have considered writing that the baby's diaper was dirty.] However on the return, "Betsy," as Mr. Gold called our machine in various humorous adjurations, came to a dead stop on a hill. It was good fun! We knew Mr. Bass was driving in behind us "to pick up the pieces," as he said. We had a merry time despite the cold.

We spent the night at the Bass headquarters at the El Tovar settlement. The housekeeper there is a woman, and we had clean sheets! The evening was very interesting. The third river scout had not been heard from, and the two haggard ones who had crawled in the night before were so nervous and queer that Mrs. Gold imagined they had deserted him. I wondered if they had killed him. They could talk of nothing but their last sight of him as they all climbed up and up, and looked meanwhile for water. They would sigh and hide their faces. They were Mormons, we heard. They told how they climbed up a fifty foot crevice of solid rock, one bracing himself and the other crawling over him, a desperate and cautious sort of leap frog. They stopped abruptly when they started to tell what it was to look down. Climbing a straight mile up!

Mr. Bass arrived cold, despite his great fur coat. After our supper we sat about a fire in another room and heard the violent conversation going on during his meal. He too, evidently felt that the men had deserted their comrade, and that they were fools not to have taken something to eat in their pockets, that a wreck could not separate from them. Such clever irony, such bold reveling I had never before heard or imagined. We couldn't help hearing.

"My straight haired Christian friend, listen to me! I'll tell you what was the matter! You left your brains in your boat with your provisions! Why didn't you have a gun in your pocket? No! Any kind of a gun! You could hit a burro. There are some down there. They have big ears. You could aim at an ear easy! Then you wouldn't starve. I know this river. I've lived thirty years by this canyon. Don't talk to me! I could have done it!" So he ran on, more and more violent whenever they interrupted.

Suddenly there was a lull. Then Bert Louzon came in and told us the third man had just come in, 48 hours without food, and a day and a half and a night without water. He had made the indescribable climb without a trail. Two days and a night he had walked steadily. Once at the top, he had followed the winding rim. It was very exciting to be there when he arrived! We went out to the kitchen-dining room and met him, and watched him eat, and heard the fresh comments. Mr. Bass was almost as hard on him as he had been on the "tenderfeet," but really was the benefactor of them all. I wish I could tell you how intensely interesting that evening was. "Old John," an ancient guide, damned things so calmly, and the poor Russel ate so steadily, and Mr. Bass commented on everything so uniquely, that Minna and I sat on the same chair and kicked each other whenever it was particularly difficult not to laugh aloud. A recording phonograph would have made our fortunes.

We slept like logs, literally. Sunday morning we walked along the rim to the lookout, when who should walk in but Miss Chapman and Philip! We were charmed to see them, and told our tale with glee. They had been spending the vacation at the hotel, and envied us accordingly. We took them back to meet Mr. Bass, and left them together when we started home. Now we have wild plans of spending a week or two with Mr. Bass in the spring vacation, or when school is out. He wants to take us to the Havasupi village down in Cataract Canyon, where the Indians are truly primitive, and still live in the cliffs. It would be overwhelmingly educational! Miss C. has a friend writing a scientific book at La Jolla with some biologist, and wants her to come, as they've always planned to be at the canyon together. Wouldn't a real camping trip like that be wonderful? Mr. Bass revels in explaining how things were made and what they are, but I think he never loses the poetry of it in the science. If Helen could join us!

At five we were home. I thot of you and of all I love most, and longed for your blessing when I saw the Canyon. As before, I found definite details lost in the overwhelming sense of the presence of God. I wish you could be there with me sometime.

Since then I have been lost in <u>Bleak House</u>. It has done me good, too. I should like to be more like Esther Summerson.

Last night Miss Chapman, Miss Watson, Grace, M., and I had supper on the hill again. We needed a larger fire than before. Of course we enjoyed it.

The girls who have been so ultra gay have one by one been getting sick and missing time at school until Mr. L. is desperate. Everyone was teaching today however.

My heart always answers your letters, even when I give no words. I love you very much. On Ruth's birthday I was uplifted, tho I dreamed, as I have over and over of finding she was gone, and waking with the feeling that it couldn't be true. She does not seem far away. I have not heard again from Mr. Craig.

Always, Your Sylvia

Williams News Dec. 2, 1915
"River Scouts Have Narrow Escape"

Charles Russel and his two assistant scouts who as announced in last week's News, attempted to descend the Colorado River from Bright Angel Trail, narrowly escaped with their lives when attempting to descend the rapids. From Bright Angel Trail it is but a few miles downstream to a course of extremely dangerous rapids. While attempting to run these the men lost their boat and felt themselves fortunate in reaching the bank with their lives.

Their boat remained afloat and little injured, held fast to some rocks far out in the stream by the force of the water. The men then tried to rescue the boat which contained all of their supplies. They passed a rope to it but so great was the force of the water that the rope snapped before appreciably affecting the boat. The two tenderfeet, at this point, seemed to have stampeded. They began a climb out of the Canyon over a course never before considered accessible and succeeded at last, footsore and near starving, in getting out of the Canyon.

Russel at last abandoned the boat and set out for the rim. He was much concerned over the safety of his two companions and endeavored to follow them but could not keep their trail. He arrived at the rim almost 24 hours later, having gone 48 hours without food or any real rest.

A rescue party returned to the boat to save its valuable cargo. It is not known how soon the trip will be continued.

Williams News, Dec. 2, 1915
"An Interesting Trip"

A number of Williams people had a most interesting trip to the Grand Canyon, recently. Mr. and Mrs. Gold and their little daughter Myra, Miss Minna Wissing and Miss Elsie Hayes left by machine, Friday morning for Bass Camp. Mr. W. W. Bass had planned to take them down his trail, at the foot of which they were to meet River Scouts and share in the motion pictures.

But man proposes and God disposes. After climbing a few trees en route, the machine arrived in the general vicinity of Bass Camp, only to lose its way, leave the splendid automobile road that leads to the camp, and come to a standstill caught on a rock.

Meanwhile, in the depths of the Canyon, the boat of river scouts was caught on another rock. However, the party from Williams finally reached the Bass Camp, heartily welcomed by their always interesting host. The view of the canyon from this point is particularly fine. A trip down the easy trail to the cliff dwellings, five hundred feet below the rim, was a delightful experience, and softened the regret over altered plans. Mr. Bass and his close and scientific knowledge of the Canyon add greatly to the pleasure of a trip there.

The party from Williams likewise returned in safety and are warmly advising their friends to visit Bass Camp.

Dec. 4, Sat. The first snowstorm of the year. I went downtown in it, and in my bountiful mail had a much appreciated letter from Mrs. Hurst. Miss W., Martha and Philip called. Washed clothes, ironed, washed hair, studied S. S. lesson, etc.

Dec. 5, Sun. Went thru the white town to S. S., and enjoyed teaching Mrs. Boone's class. St. Jenkins, the archdeacon, gave an inspiring sermon, communion. We had dinner at the Gold's, and enjoyed them. Myra is adorable, wrote letters, particularly to Edna. I constantly make new resolves.

Dec. 6, Mon. Wrote business letters, read in <u>David Copperfield</u>.

Dec. 7, Tues. Debated in English lit. Women's Club at Parish House after problems at school. Down town with the girls. Finished <u>Bleak House</u>, helped by its wholesome philosophy

Dec. 8, Wed. Tried to let this day uplift me, as Alice said. How often I have thought of my Ruthie to-day [anniversary of her death]! I am blest in memory

Dec. 9, Thurs. Better relations with Minnie and Easter make me glad (both hard to manage). Accomplished a great deal, doing extra school work, making out questions on <u>Silas Marner</u>, exam questions, planning ahead, etc. Snow melting.

Dec. 10, Fri. Memories come to me, but I am uplifted. Love is eternal, and one can grow worthier of it, and go on. Went with Miss Watson to basketball games. Her brother took us home, and I had a pleasant evening there.

Dec. 11, Sat. Washed and ironed clothes, cleaned two rooms, read in <u>David Copperfield</u>, wrapped Christmas gifts. Heard I am probably to go to Long Beach for all my holidays.

Dec. 12, Sun. Taught the S. S. class again. Another fine sermon on "The Coming of the Kingdom of God" by the Archdeacon. Wrote letters. Trying not to let my cold make me ill.

Dec. 13, Mon. Cold better. Such busy days at school! Went with Mildred to see about Christmas rates.

Dec. 14, Tues. Snowing again. Went to Women's Club with Miss Chapman, discussion of Rostand. Wrapped gifts, both Minna and I, all the evening. Enjoyed it. Finished careful and delightful reading of <u>David Copperfield</u>.

Dec. 15, Wed. Good papers on <u>Silas Marner</u> from English I. Reread (skimmed) <u>The Marble Faun</u>.

Dec. 16, Thurs. Minna found she has an unexpected niece, and the dear girl is overwhelmed with gladness. I received my lovely picture of my niece and her parents, and revel in it. I am so eager, so excited over going home! Supper at the Sines', snow wonderful.

Dec. 17, Fri. The snow is fascinating. Refused invitations to coast because of my cold. Examinations close the fourth month. Corrected papers. Sewed on Mrs. Gold's machine.

Dec. 18, Sat. Minna is very happy. Her family have relented. Corrected papers. Went with Mildred, Miss Chapman and Philip to reserve berths. Oh I am happy over going home! Washed and cleaned. Then Miss C., Minna and I went in the snow for pine branches.

Dec. 19, Sun. Church did me good. I prepared our dinner at home. Tramped thru the canyon some distance, in the snow with Miss C. and Miss W. Beautiful! Wrapped gifts and wrote letters!

Dec. 20, Mon. Christmas excitement at school, and carols sung in rehearsal for Municipal Tree. Miss W. and we went to Miss Chapman's for evening.

Dec. 21, Tues. Still busy with grades etc. A group of us went downtown together after school.

Dec. 22, Wed. Rehearsals have made the children too excited for much work. Stopped briefly at the Sweetwoods', Watson's, and Mrs. Whiting's. Preparations for departure.

Dec. 23, Thurs. California train. Rose early, half day of school. Travelling with Mildred Murphy, Miss Chapman and Philip. At Ash Fork met and talked with Mable Lee and Glen Girdner of Oak Creek and with Eloise Bartlett. Visited later on train with E. B. How glad I am to be in Calif., and going home.

Dec. 24, Fri. 316 Winchester Drive, Long Beach, Calif. Saw Claremont from berth. Met by Father and Hylinda in L.A., and shopped with Hylinda. Home about noon, happy to be with family, all 18 of us together. Dorothy more charming than ever. Decorated house and helped with tree. So glad to be here!

Dec. 25, Sat. Dorothy in bed with me while I looked at my stocking. Then soon the tree and many lovely gifts. Dinner and then auto ride and talks. I make the most of the love of friends and dear family. That is very much!

Dec. 26, Sun. While others were at church I stayed with the dear baby, helped her play, gave her a bottle, took her driving. Went with Alice and to call on Harnetts and Morris family. Went to Christian Church with Aunt Mamie and Alice to hear Ernest sing.

Dec. 27, Mon. Helped mother buy a coat, and with Hylinda helped Ernest wash communion glasses. Went to L.A., shopped largely for other people. Too tired to telephone other friends.

Dec. 28, Tues. All the family went by machine to Alhambra, to Uncle Board's for a reunion dinner. Lovely day.

Dec. 29, Wed. Christmas greetings still coming, "embarrass me with riches" as Aunt Mamie might say. Still have cold etc.; but have had happy day with the family, playing with baby, helping with housework, talking.

Dec. 30, Thurs. Helped to clean the house etc. Spend much time with Dorothy. Helen came in afternoon, and we took Dorothy out for a ride. Talked late with her. Good to have her with me again.

Dec. 31, Fri. Took Helen to car about seven A.M. Helped Alice wash etc. and did some work for myself, and phoning. Went with Hylinda to call on Mrs. Rallier, with whom she may go to Africa. Talked in bed intimately with mother, and am glad I can do.

Jan. 1, 1916, Sat. Long Beach Calif. to Arizona by train. Packed suitcases; watched the dear baby in her bath. Big relative dinner given by

Aunt Mary Hylinda went with me in rain to Los Angeles and we called on Staileys, saw Ruth's things, wondered when I should see Helen again, and life seemed unreal. Hated to leave my family and friends.

Jan. 2, Sun. Williams. Again wrote thank-yous on the train. Met by Minna. Took flowers to Mrs. Whiting, the Watsons, and the Golds. Gifts awaiting me. Touched by one from Mrs. Hurst. I will try to make the new year a good one.

Jan. 3, Mon. Took California flowers to the Sines and to Mrs. Parker; took shopping to the Watsons.

Jan. 5, Wed. Went with Miss W. and her brother to a dance in honor of Margaret Dermont. Really enjoyed it. I'm too much of a hermit!

Jan. 8, Sat. Mary and Georgia moved in next door. Went with Sugar and Minna to movies, followed by Santa Fe concert, Texas orchestra. Stayed for part of dance. Added later: Met John John Planwydd Roberts for the first time then.

Jan. 9, Sun. Went to church and with Minna to Dr. Melick's for dinner. Trying to be cheerful, and to adjust myself.

Jan.10, Mon. M. and I floundered thru deep snow and a wild storm to the Watson's! Pleasant evening. Guided home by the brother.

Jan. 11, Tues. Reviewing strenuously for semester examinations. At Women's Club I reviewed D'Annunzio's Daughter of Joris. Pleased by praise. Town with Mr. Boone. A year is a long time. I must push on.

10

Threads of My Life

Thou shalt know Him when
He comes, Not by any din of
drums. Nor by the vantage of His
airs, Nor by anything He wears.
Neither by His crown, Nor His gown.
For His presence known shall be
By the holy harmony Which His
coming makes in thee.
—Anonymous

By November of 1915 Elsie found herself identifying with Esther Summerson of Dickens's *Bleak House*, who seemed to have a trust that God was ordering the events of her tragic life. Perhaps Elsie, the writer and reader, could not help but allow her decisions and actions to be influenced by the very books she could not live without.

Elsie's trip to the Grand Canyon seemed to be a turning point in her attitude. She wrote to her sister that she "found details lost in the overwhelming sense of the presence of God." Awed by the glory of the canyon, she seemed to find peace with the death of Ruth and perhaps even the loss of a future with Karl.

This peace would allow her emotionally to move on, perhaps even to a new love. Elsie describes "a wild blizzard" the night of her first date with a gentleman named Jack Roberts, and that is just about how he blew into her life.

Jan. 12, 1916, Wed. After school a group of us went to watch skiing. Talked with Minna about our affairs of the heart until midnight.

Jan. 14, Fri. Monthly exams for grades. Corrected some of my papers. Downtown in a wild snowstorm and bitter wind with Miss Watson and Minna.

Jan. 15, Sat. Corrected papers. Minna counted 13 people as coming to the house today! Miss Watson and Mrs. Parker called, children came to see about grades, etc. Agent brought my 25 volumes of Dickens for which I paid $17.00 cash, "special price." Downtown with Mrs. Walker who took me to lunch and to see <u>Foolish Virgin</u>.

Jan. 16, Sun. Snow falling all day. Few at church.

Jan. 17, Mon. Rain melting the snow. Still correcting papers. Minna, Miss W. and I "dropped in" at the Chapman's, and had a pleasant evening. Read absurd "literature" there.

Jan. 18, Tues. Rain by day, and wild wind at night. Made out grades. Axel came for a lesson in English from Minna. Studied. Read some of Bryant's poems.

Letter from Elsie's mother
Long Beach
Jan. 19, 1916

My Sweet Elsie,

We received a postal from you Monday p.m. I hate to think how deep the snow must be at Williams by this time. Except Saturday it has rained almost constantly since Friday. Great damage has been done by high water, floods, etc. The large bridge going to Los Angeles was carried away last night. Long Beach is cut off from L.A. except going by water to San Pedro. Great loss of property in lowlands, homes washed away and some deaths by drowning.

I was to see Hylinda for a few minutes yesterday. She works hard for the $1.00 a day.

It will be great fun for you to learn to ski.

I love you very much and thank God for you.

Mama

Jan. 19, Wed. Mail delayed by heavy floods. Corrected notebooks. Began looking over <u>Tale of Two Cities</u>. Later finished it skimming. Began preparations for University work next year [at Berkeley].

Jan. 20, Thurs. Thought of Aunt Mamie on her birthday; but still no mail can go or come. Mr. L. had a long talk with me, and visited a class. I want to do better work. Corrected themes.

Jan. 21, Fri. Went with Georgia and Dorothy Savage to a High School party. Enjoyed cards and dancing, washing the dishes later, talking with the children and helping to take a group of the girls home. It is now 2 A.M. I am waiting for hot water for foot water.

Jan. 22, Sat. Lovely birthday remembrances from home. Minna as a "surprise" had the Drop-In Club for supper. Lovely time. A day that made me glad and uplifted.

Jan. 23, Sun. Went to church. We had our dinner at home. Walked with the girls to the dam. Read in <u>Mill on the Floss</u>.

Elsie at Bill Williams Dam

Jan. 24, Mon. Walked with Mrs. Gold and Myra after school. Mrs. Plummer asked me to a "reading" before the public! Sorry to decline.

Jan. 25, Tues. Talked with Axel (the young Swede whom Minna is teaching English), for an hour or so while she was gone. Read in <u>Mill on the Floss</u>.

Jan. 27, Thurs. Simply lost in <u>Mill on the Floss</u>, in Maggie's identity, when about Nine P.M. Mr. Roberts and Ed Maliss came to take us to League party. Storm had made us decide to stay home; but we went. Wild blizzard; Minna and I sleep together because house may blow over to night.

Jan. 28, Fri. Plunged through snowdrifts. Mr. Roberts cleaned our paths and came on errands. Went with Mary and Mr. Sweeny to dance and card party. Enjoyed it. Home at 3 A.M.

Jan. 29, Sat. Rose at 11:30 A.M. (disgusted with William's hours) and went after my carnations won as a card prize last night and left at Parish House! We went with Mr. Roberts to choir practice. Interesting talks with Mr. R. who is Welsh, nephew of David Lloyd George [Prime Minister of England].

Teachers posing on a snag (left) John John Planwydd Roberts (right)

Jan. 30, Sun. Plunged through the snow to church. We walked with Mr. Roberts to the dam, took pictures. Planning to visit Mrs. Hurst at Oak Creek.

Feb. 1, Tues. Went with Mabyn Chapman to the Women's Club meeting. Went with them to the pictures, <u>Helene of the North</u>. Coming home in cold across the snow I told her much. She is lovely Wrote to Alice M. Parker.

Feb. 2, Wed. Felt ill, so that school was hard work. Went to bed rather early

Feb. 3, Thurs. Again did not feel equal to skiing. Almost lost my voice.

Feb. 4, Fri. Left before school was out, and came home. Began <u>Ivanhoe</u>. Went to bed, ill.

Feb. 5, Sat. Spent a good part of day in bed. Grip, or just worn-out? Mildred and Miss Mitchell and Miss Chapman and Mary called. Also Mr. Roberts, pockets full of bottles of fruit juice for me!

Feb. 6, Sun. Still staying much in bed, and so re-reading <u>Ivanhoe</u>. I sat in glorious sunshine on back porch.

Feb. 7, Mon. Stayed home from school. Sense of spiritual fever gone, and I feel far better in body too. Finished <u>Ivanhoe</u>, enjoying it much more than I used to. Began Green's <u>History of the English People</u>. Mr. R. brought his arms full again.

Feb. 8, Tues. Better, but still wobbly and still out of school. Did school work in sun again. People are very kind! Miss W. and Miss C. each brought custard, and Mr. Roberts fresh eggs! Mr. Udine sent fruit, and Mrs. Drennan cake.

Feb. 9, Wed. Rose late, and at noon went back to school. Appreciated the welcome given me. Read London's <u>South Sea Tales</u>, vivid with pictures and horror.

Feb. 10, Thurs. Decidedly better. At school all day. Miss C. helped me plan for Berkeley. Minna's ring came, and she is radiantly happy.

Feb. 11, Fri. Glorious spring weather. Monthly exams. Georgia kindly kept assembly all day. Read London's <u>Call of the Wild</u>. Refused to go to party with M. and Mr. R; not yet quite strong.

Feb. 12, Sat. Mildred brought us tangerines from home before I was up. Letter from Mrs. Hurst. Mr. Roberts called.

Feb 13, Sun. Stayed home from church, but went for a walk up the track with Minna and Mr. Roberts. Received more valentines!

Feb. 14, Mon. Still glorious spring weather. Sat long in the sun on the Watson's porch, talking.

Feb. 17, Thurs. Began preparations for first regular debate, combining Eng. I and Eng. II. Came home early and washed. Martha called, and Mrs. Sine called later, bringing cake and sherbet. Refused a party, though Mr. Roberts came for us.

Feb. 18, Fri. Swept two rooms after school. Minna and I went with Mr. Roberts to Epworth League party. Had a good time. Treated Mr. Fortney naturally at last.

Feb. 19, Sat. Rose late in order to rest. Sugar came and took me to the show. Robert Warnick in <u>The Stolen Voice</u>. Enjoyed it.

Feb. 20, Sun. Wrote to 20 people! (Chiefly cards to Cornville children.) Sat in sun on porch. Went with Jack Roberts and Minna to Methodist League and Episcopal Church. We had a little supper here afterward. Sat in the sun on porch.

Feb. 21, Mon. Rain and snow alternating. Received an angel-food cake from my dear mother. We went for the first time to Mrs. Parker's for dinner, largely a men's boarding-house!

Feb. 22, Tues. Jack brought ice-cream after supper, and we went with him to picture show and Santa Fe afterward that was not much good. He plans to go to Clarkdale with me!

Feb. 24, Thurs. Debate in Eng II and III, "The Allies have a better chance of winning etc." Mr. Roberts took our Drop-In Club to the box factory and tried to teach Mary Collins and me Welsh a bit!

Feb. 25, Fri. Thought of Father on his birthday. Excitement because the rest of the Board have tried to oust Mrs. Miller. Hear nice things about debate. M. and I went to dinner at the Golds' and talked with Mr. Bass, another guest, about Canyon plans. Wonderful invitation for a trip to Indian villages, moving pictures, etc.

Feb. 26, Sat. Washed clothes, pressed, mended, renovated clothes. Jack came, but I wouldn't go the movies, play too sad. We went downtown, bought ice cream, etc., and at home cut out red hearts for the party.

Feb. 27, Sun. We went to dinner at Fray Marcos with Jack. Prepared to lead League, and led it, subject "character." Then went with J. to my own church.

Feb. 28, Mon. Told Mr. Latham I do not expect to be here next year, and he said pleasant things. Finished reading <u>The Lady of the Lake</u>.

Feb. 29, Tues. This time I can't note what I did one or two years ago today! [Leap year.]

Went with Jack to see <u>Peer Gynt</u> in pictures (Cyril Maude star) and afterward a really excellent Kansas Santa Fe! It was the DeTar Co. Jolly time.

March 1, Wed. March came in "like a lion." Almost blizzard. Minna, Miss C. and I talked after school, after Minna showed Miss C. her diamond. Jack tried to teach us to roller skate. We amuse ourselves with foolishness.

March 3, Fri. Went with Jack Roberts and Minna to choir practice and then to skating party! Had hosts of fun. Letter from Mrs. Hurst telling me floods may be high last of month. Shall I go to her then?

March 4, Sat. Spent much of the afternoon at M. C.'s. She did me a great deal of good. Jack came, and we had supper together. He stayed late helping us cut red hearts, make rhymes, etc. The nonsense between us is refreshing.

Jack's rhymes:

I'm studious Elsie as you all know well;
The papers I've graded I ne'er could tell
The saying you know, "Every Dog has his turn."
How I'm to have mine you soon will learn
For next year in Berkeley, to live is my hope
And there let the other fellow Grade My Dope.
Germans, English and the French
They are all Bad foes to fight
But it is quite evident
That the Welsh you win at sight

(Apologies if our war correspondent seems confused.)

In the wilds of Arizona where girls have such winning ways
There once lived a fair young maiden and her name was Elsie Hayes
But her partner she got married and so left her all alone
So the dear little damsel swore she'd call some man her own
And she fished and looked so dainty that a fellow couldn't wait
Did you ever know a sucker who'd not fall for such sweet bait.

Planwydd

March 5, 1916 Sun. Communion, the morning service. Jack took us to League and then to Miss C's by invitation. Miss C. played and Jack sang. He also read us one of Lady Gregory's plays, <u>Spreading the News</u>, in dialect.

March 6, Mon. Hurt my hand, and J. played doctor! Martha S. and he helped with party preparations until late again. More foolishness.

March 7, Tues. Thought of my niece on her first birthday. Georgia and I gave the announcement party for Minna and Mary (J. helped again). Red hearts, red carnations, heart tallies, hearts game, heart ice cream, heart boxes with favors and rhymes, Minna and Mary having rings in theirs.

March 8, Wed. Nice things about my going said to me, as well as good wishes galore given to Minna. Went with Jack to League surprise party for Lulu M. and Martha M. Mr. Fortney made me wish he hadn't, yet I like him. Home late again.

March 9, Thurs. School. Mrs. Boone called, bringing sandwiches. I shopped by mail.

March 10, Fri. Monthly examinations. Packed the pink box I decorated yesterday, and took it to the Box Social to which I went with Jack. Saw a good deal of Mr. Fortney. Children called.

March 11, Sat. A. M. Chapman called, and told us of her happy plans. I am more than glad for her. Went with Jack to pictures, Nash in <u>Cotton King</u>.

March 12, Sun. Taught Mary's S. S. class of dear, wee tots. Wrote letters out-of-doors. Went to league and to church with Jack. He brought ice-cream, and we talked late.

March 15, Wed. Jack came to supper. We started to church, but I lost my gold acorn and looked for it until too late. J. helped me make out averages and put them on report cards. Vaguely disturbed for fear he may be getting serious.

March 16, Thurs. Debate on Preparedness. In bed read practically all of Allen Raine's <u>By Berwen Banks</u>, the Welsh tale from Jack.

March 17, Fri. Teachers meeting. "Drop-Ins" met at the Watsons. Roy Watson and Jack were there. Walk and talk with Mr. Fortney at noon.

March 18, Sat. Washed clothes, received and answered letter from Mrs. Hurst, trying to plan my arrival. Went to see Mary Pickford as Cinderella. Charming! Horrid headache. Went to bed. Rose for the evening, and told Jack I wouldn't go out with him. Then Mr. Bolger, the Harnetts' cousin, called with a letter of introduction. I enjoyed him.

March 19, Sun. About 7 we went for a picnic breakfast beyond the dam. Fires for various couples, I with Jack! Went in afternoon for long tramp on hills with him and to church at night. Wrote home and to Alice M. Parker and Helen about him!

March 20, Mon. Went with Jack to see William Faversham in Parker's Right of Way, and the Auracher Concert Co., a Santa Fe, came afterward. Showed him pictures and article on his uncle, Lloyd George, and pictures of my family and friends. What am I going to do with him?

March 21, Tues. Women's Club. Jack refused to read to the Club. Jack came to help me work on my Kodak book.

March 22, Wed. Bad weather makes me doubt whether I can go to Oak Creek.

March 23, Thurs. Snow again, and I'm practically sure I can't cross the streams. Wrote to Mrs. Hurst to say so. Then I believe it is best not to go, since I can't evidently Letter from Alice M. Parker about emphasis of my visit there. Went to church with Jack. Reviewed some Latin and French with him.

March 24, Fri. Strange thoughts of Oak Creek since I can't go. Got sawdust in my eye bringing in wood and got a horrid headache from my eyes. Mr. Earl Fortney called and borrowed books. Went with Jack and Minna to choir practice. Jack showed sympathy!

March 25, Sat. [39] Eyes still bad, rose late then went downtown. Talked with Minna about Jesse and Jack and marriage! Jack brought another box

---

39 On this day in Phoenix Karl Hurst enlisted in Co. 1 1st Arizona Infantry, Arizona National Guard. His questionnaire asked if he had ever been hospitalized for mental illness and he entered "no." On May 9, 1916, as a result of raids on American border towns by the Mexican revolutionary Pancho Villa, the First Arizona Infantry was called into federal service as part of US Forces stationed on the Mexican border under command of General John J. Pershing. Designated the 158th Infantry Regiment on August 5,1917, the regiment served in France during WWI as part of the 40th Infantry Division. (http://azmemory.lib.az.us/cdm4/index.php?CISOROOT=/ammbush).

of cactus candy because of the legend that goes with it![40] I tried in vain to make him dignified.

March 26, Sun. A special day! Walked through the canyon with Jack, would not go to church because of my eyes. And then he told me he loves me! I am dazed, and feel in a dream. I hope I can love him.

March 27, Mon. Week of spring vacation. Rose late, to rest my eyes, pinched myself to see if I am awake! Got dinner for Jack. We walked a little. Oh I don't want to hurt him more!

March 28, Tues. Started a Hope Chest! Lay down and covered my eyes while others sewed. Missed Jack in the evening.

Box 315, Williams
March 28, 1916

Dearest Mother:

Your good letter came to me here. As I wrote you, the streams were high. However, since about Sat. the weather has been beautiful, and I have enjoyed the freedom. I really needed a vacation, especially my eyes.

I am putting in a picture of the suit I want of blue linen. I certainly will be grateful if you will make it. I'll send the pattern if I can get one here. I am ordering the linen sent to you from Los Angeles. I shouldn't think this style would be hard to make. I'll tell you later about length and buttons and belt. Don't you think it would be best to have the black silk left off the collar, because of laundering? I wish there could be a touch of black besides the belt though.

Do get a new hat, mother, dear. You've surely worn your old one long enough! The crepe dress must be pretty. The cleaning of the pipe must have been a good job. I'm glad Aunt Mamie got a skirt.

---

40 "The first makers of cactus candy were supposed to be the Toltecs. They believed that there was imprisoned within the Visnaga cactus the soul of a beautiful maiden. The thorns were believed to protect her purity. A young man would bring the choicest specimen of this cactus to the home of the parents of the bride-elect. After the candy was made the bride and groom would be bound together by consuming a piece of cactus candy, while their lips met" (advertisement for Donofrio's Crystallized Cactus Candy, Phoenix, AZ).

Commencement at Pomona begins the 17th of June and school is out here the 2nd. The Canyon trip may not materialize, but I'll probably visit Mrs. Hurst then before I leave Arizona. I'll have a big box of freight or express, chiefly books and bedding. To what place shall I have it sent? And where shall I send my trunk? I probably shall not go to Berkeley the first semester, partly to rest my eyes and the rest of me first, and partly because I might care enough for Jack not to go at all. By December I ought to know. If I were going to be married soon, of course, I'd want to be home instead of at the University in the time between. Please don't mention this outside the family! Jack has persuaded me to do this, tho he understands perfectly, that at present I can make no promises. It certainly is a problem. I'm afraid he'll just feel worse all the time if I let him go on, but I really wish I could care enough for him.

I keep wondering what you would think of him, and what his parents would think of me. They are evidently very well bred and well educated, and fine people in every way. But Jack has lived so long in Canada and Alaska that he says he hardly knows how to behave in "civilization" now, and his English certainly has been corrupted! He's going to try to use again orally the perfect English he still writes. Of course, it's a foreign tongue to him. Also he's trying to stop smoking, though I've never asked him to, and it really doesn't matter seriously to me. He's a Presbyterian though, like me, he's accustomed to the Episcopal Church and likes it very much. He knows the service well. He goes there often with me at night, and mornings to the M.E. Church. He is one of those remarkably rare individuals of the present generation, a young man who goes regularly to church and is not ashamed of being "religious," and yet is absolutely anything rather than effeminate. I've been getting better acquainted with some of the other men here, and Jack surely is their superior. Those who don't go to church are evidently trivial, and those who do, except Jack, are, I at least fear less desirable in the long run than those who don't! They are what in slang we call "mutts!" Earl Fortney, for instance, a young ex high school teacher now in the Forest Service, who called the other day, and with whom I'm probably going to church next Sunday, he is President of the Epworth League and, like Jack (who is also an Epworth League Officer), sings in the

Methodist choir. But, altho he's well read and a good talker and wide awake and all that, I almost despise him sometimes. I think he's both girlish and sentimental, despite his really particularly good qualities. Of course this isn't a typical town, but I do think Jack is an unusually fine specimen of manhood. He's over a year younger than I, but seems older. We are wonderfully congenial in most ways.

He says he'll give me time to think, and he'll secure a position in Southern California about the time I leave here, and then he'll bring a diamond if I'll let him.

Jack is thoroughly Americanized, except for his accent, and has taken out his papers. He says he knows he will never live in Wales again and unless I refuse him he'll never go back to the wilds. It is very tempting to think of living near the rest of you, with a home of my own, and no more fear of wearing out in school teaching, and a man to take care of me and love me the rest of my life. So I have to be careful not to over-estimate that side of it, and my desire not to hurt him, and so consent when I might not really care enough for him. He says he ought to get $150 a month in California, tho he might not be able immediately to get what he wants. He wants to have charge of a lumber yard in some small town. Here he directs a gang of Mexicans and Greeks at the mill, grading lumber, etc. He has worked six years before this with the largest, or one of the largest, lumber companies in this country. However, they do not include California in this territory, and he thinks it would please me for him to settle there. He evidently had a very good position with them, and can get the best of recommendations. Then for about three years he lived on the homestead he took up in Canada. I believe 160 miles from the railroad when he first went there. Because his family had influence and he had unusual ability or interest in his studies he was admitted to a Welsh University when he was about fifteen. He studied so hard that his family sent him over here with an uncle for a brief change, but here he has stayed about ten years. Minna admires him tremendously. I really think from what she has said that if it hadn't been for Jesse she would have wanted Jack to fall in love with her! You'll probably see him soon after school is out unless I repudiate him altogether before then. Anyway, I'm going to start a Hope Chest again! I told him frankly about Karl, but he said that didn't change his feeling for me, and he's willing to wait to see if I can learn to care for him. I wish I could! He has been so indifferent to girls that his friends have called him a woman hater! When he first began calling he remarked frequently that he never expected to marry. I don't see why he should so suddenly have fallen in love with me, when he's never loved before. He certainly takes it hard. He is amused himself to think of how he's gone serenely all over North America, more or less, while his friends tried vainly to get him interested in girls, and then in this town should fall in love!

Please send my old elk hide mountain shoes. They may be in a box in the milk house. I'll pay postage, and also on these last eggs. How much were they? I always destroy the cover before I think of noticing the amount. I want to be out of doors as much as I can, now, and probably Jack and I will tramp every clear Sunday afternoon. Of course we'll go with a group when we go far. There's to be another breakfast outside next Sunday. I think that's fine. Everybody gets back in time for Sunday school. Jack's living with Mr. Hoffpauir, the Methodist minister, now.

We are to have lunch with Miss C., Miss W. going, too, and each furnishing something. It's about time to go. I've chiefly rested so far this vacation and seen Jack!

With much love, Elsie

March 29, Wed. Went with nine of my girls (Minnie, Pauline, Vivia, 2 Mildreds, Kathryn, Riola, Lenore, and Dorothy) on a glorious picnic across the stream in the canyon and by a wild cliff. Went with Lulu later and chose 2 Indian baskets for Minna and bought a Canyon spoon for my own Hope Chest! To church with Jack. Then we made a compact! I hope more.

March 30, Thurs. Wrote some letters, dropped in at Miss Watson's. M. and I went to stay all night with Mildred, Martha and Lulu. There a sudden surprise party came, presenting Minna with the Indian baskets Lulu and I had chosen. Missed saying "goodnight" to Jack alone!

March 31, Fri. Remade my hat at the girls, then came home and trimmed it. Jose brought a note from Jack saying he is ill. I tried not to worry, but wrote him, and we sent a foot-warmer! Then I looked up Mr. Fortney and asked him to go look after Jack and gave him some soup for him. Mr. Gold called and we talked of wretched school affairs. Earl called to report Jack better, and I'm much relieved. I think I'll care enough!

Letter from Elsie's mother
Fri. evening March 31, 1916

My Dear Elsie:

Your <u>very</u> interesting letter received yesterday From what you have told us of Jack he must be fine. It seems odd to me that you don't know whether you like him well enough. As to what we think of him or his people think of you is a very secondary matter seems to me. You are old enough to choose and if you love him, and he surely seems to love you that ought to settle it. I know it is a serious thing, marriage always is. But ordinarily when two Christian people love each other it ought to be right and proper for them to marry It would make me very happy to see you married to a good man whom you loved. I surely hate to think of you teaching all your life.

I am so sorry your eyes are troubling you! Just write us postal cards unless there is something special to tell us.

The pattern came, is pretty and I don't think will be hard to make. I hope to work on it next week, as it is Aunt M.'s week to cook.

We have 127 little chicks and 8 little turkeys, my special chore to feed and water them, takes quite a bit of time.

I expect to send your shoes if Papa goes to town tomorrow. Postage on last eggs was 15 cents. I should think you would want your freight sent here as long as it is our home, and will be until we are lucky enough to find a better place.

You could explain to Jack that Papa is better here, that we are experimenting with the chicken business and may not stay here long. I am just awful sorry you haven't a nicer home to invite him to, but we will have to make the best of it. I want you to spend most of your summer at the beach, but suppose you would want him to visit us all here, so he could see us and we him.

Saturday, after dinner Papa and I are taking our rests, then expect to go to town.

Much Love, Mama

April 1, Sat. Jack and I had wonderful afternoon climbing in the canyon and talking at the foot of the cliffs where the children and I went Wed. He took me to the Golds' dinner party for father Gold at night. I care more and more. But I did not forget.

April 2, Sun. I can't say how glad I am. I am almost the same as engaged to Jack. It seems more dream-like yet to see it written. Church and League, and between Jack here to dinner and a wonderful afternoon in the forest again; and afterward at home. I respect Jack more than ever after our intimate talking.

April 3, Mon. School again after the vacation. Talked with Minna about Jack. Darned stockings, etc. He's having a music lesson!

Letter from Aunt Mamie

Dearest 1,

I am glad that U liked & enjoyed the flowers. Wish U could C my garden now, 29 big red poppies R in bloom and petunias galore, pansies, & snapdragons. I Njoy them all, I am so glad Jack is fond of mignonette, it shows a refined taste, I have an idea that "Jack" & I will B like brothers, (as it were) when once we become acquainted.

Yes, I think Roberts is a good last name, & I like Jack. How kind that he will "share the heather" with me, I never saw any, but having some Scotch rubbed into me, I will appreciate it much. I shall be sure to like him Elsie. I hope he loves you with all his heart & that U love him with all yours. Else, I don't intend 2 give my blessing! Well, I struggle with grammar myself, so I sympathize with him. U know my slips! 1 article 4 your Hope Chest is a dainty work apron, with pockets 4 your fancy work, it has embroidered on it "How doth the little Missy Bee" & then five bees are flying on it, it has pink chain stitch dripping up and down. Then a handkerchief with the finest tatting on it I ever saw, made by an old schoolmate of your Aunt Annie's, and laid by 4 U, my own love, it is the single kind, but so fine, when cousin Mattie was here, she raved over it, and she tatted much herself! Said she "never saw any so fine", it is yours. I intend 2 give U $25.00 as I did Alice, and make a darned net 4 a set of underclothes 4 U.

I love you very hard. I hope U will get that diamond soon, & Njoy it now while your love is new, why not? Don't put off the wedding day very long, lest U should have to say with Evangeline, in the poem, "Ah, lost days & nights, when we might have been happy." Much love 2 U & Minna, I hope U told Jack how nice I am!

Loving, Aunt Mamie

April 4, Tues. I live in a dream-world. It doesn't seem more real than the imaginings of Fan and Eleanor and I in the eighth grade, except sometimes when Jack is with me! Jack doing Epworth League work tonight. Minnie D. told him I was ill, in mischief! In one month how life has changed for me! Indeed I shall not forget him. I think we shall spend the rest of our lives together.

April 5, Wed. After school Earl Fortney made a long call, and some children brought baby rabbits for us to see. Went to church with Jack, and made plans with him afterward. I kissed Jack, because I love him. I am glad.

April 6, Thur. Stayed home from "Drop-Ins" to rest eyes and go early to bed. Is this gladness really mine?

April 7, Fri. Downtown with M. C. then Philip came for a hand-out and locked me in the woodshed. Went with Jack to Epworth League social. We came home early because his cold had settled in a tooth. Poor boy! I wish I knew.

April 8, Sat. Mabyn, Minna and I visited Mexican and Spanish towns and ordered crocheting alike for pillowslips. So fun, especially when they guessed! Martha and little Myra here, Jack and I played with Myra!

April 9, Sun. Before seven went by the dam for a group breakfast. Jack and I from before three until after seven tramped in the wilds, following a stream beyond the dams, glorious! After church he came to supper. He sang "The End of a Perfect Day," and I agreed. It was wonderful.

April 10, Mon. Planned third inter-class debate, this one on success of administration. Sent for our recipe files Jack is giving Minna and me! He is taking his music lesson to-night. Wrote long letter to Mrs. Hurst.

April 11, Tues. Struggles in discipline. To the Moores' for a dinner-party, Jack came for me, and we came back to "Arcadia" for the most of the evening. He gave me a Williams spoon.

April 12, Wed. Called on Mrs. Boone, had tea there, and talked intimately. I wish I had known her better before.

Letter from Alice, Elsie's sister
April 12, 1916

Dear Elsie,

    I must scribble a few lines to tell you how very happy the news makes us. We think it is all perfectly lovely. I do wish I knew "him", but then I suppose we shall before so very long. By the way you've never told us what he looks like! Nor where he expects to abide, etc. Is he blonde or dashing brunette? Is he literary, athletic, musical or just "nothing special" like me? If he intends taking you away from California he'd better not show up at all, or we won't let him get away.

    Here I've been hoping against hope that some one of my friends would get married so we would have tastes in common (you don't know what a difference it makes) and then here comes along my own sister to obligingly fill the gap!

    You know I've been thinking lately that you and I had become much more congenial than we used to be and now with such a bond we ought to be the best chums in the world. For I think that "the best husband that ever lived" for one's very own is one of God's very richest gifts. I say one of them, for I wouldn't put any gift above that of our dear baby.

I feel horribly out of it if all the preparations have to go on up at Elsinore while I'm here, even if I might be able to help from afar a trifle.

Another thing you haven't given us an idea of is the date. I suppose Berkeley will be given up as that would mean two years if you made any use of your right to teach H.S. and that's far too long! My, won't it be great to have a brother! And for Dorothy to have an uncle will be fine!

Dorothy springs some new dear little "stunt" most every day. Yesterday when I took her up from her nap she reached right for my cheek and gave me a resounding smack of a kiss. Francis was over in the p.m. and we were discussing going for a walk. D. apparently took it all in for she said "bye, bye" and went right over to the carriage which she pulled back and forth.

When I heard the news I felt as if I'd like to tell "him" how glad I was but I guess you can convey my ideas along that line to him better than I.

Lovingly & with the best
of good wishes, Alice

April 13, Thurs. Went to movies with Jack, Bosworth in <u>The Little Brother of the Rich</u>; and a Santa Fe afterward by a Catholic school. Not much good, but I enjoy my escort!

April 14, Fri. After school helped Mrs. Gold get ready for the Ladies Aid recipe shower she has planned for Minna. In the evening Jack helped carry dishes there, etc.

April 14, 1916

Dearest Alice,

As evidently you did not receive some of the statements I sent home I'll try to answer some of your questions! Your dear letter was very welcome. Your interest and gladness for me adds a great deal to my joy.

No, I don't expect now to go to Berkeley. My idea at present is that I'll spend a little time only at Elsinore this summer, while it's so hot, but spend the fall there. I may get an apartment at Long Beach for a month or two, having some of the family with me. I'll surely hope to be with you, or have you with me, often this summer, even if you are at Westminster. Very likely we shall be married next winter, altho I feel that is uncertain as yet!

Jack is in the lumber business, and expects, because my family are there, to settle in Southern California. It may be several months before he is permanently located there, and he doesn't know of course just where it will be. He expects to get a position in Los Angeles when I leave here.

As to his looks and tastes, both are a curious mixture of the Celtic and the American, the cultured and the elemental.

I'll be as frank as Mamie was about Arthur! He looks Welsh, and he's very much tanned, and he was so nearly killed once in hockey that some false teeth (!) are one remaining effect of the excitement. He's more than a year younger than I, but I think looks older. He has very thick, straight, dark hair, but particularly nice blue eyes. Sometimes I think he's very odd looking and sometimes I think he's very good-looking. He always looks good-natured.

He entered a Welsh university when he was fourteen or fifteen, because his family have "pull," he says, but I think also because he did unusual work! He studied so much that his parents sent him here on a trip when he was about sixteen, and here he's been ever since. English is of course a foreign language for him, and tho he learned it correctly from his governess and at school, he has acquired so much slang and peculiar grammar in the wilds and in his work of directing more foreign foreigners that he's having a struggle to try to improve it now that he expects to live in "civilization" again, and to marry me! By this time he thinks in English, though.

He's a natural linguist, and picks up every language dialect and vocabulary generally that he hears. He was taught French and Latin and English I think almost as soon as Welsh! He knows Irish and Scotch dialects to perfection, and sings in them as well as speaks in them when he wants to do it.

He is very entertaining, with a good voice, quick Celtic wit, and spontaneous merry-heartedness. He is rather shy with strangers because of his years away from civilization, but evidently did not have that quality in the least before, so will probably get over it.

Of course I like him, but so does everybody else! We are very congenial. He likes books; and the out-of-doors particularly. He's a Presbyterian, but he likes the "Church of England," as he calls the Episcopal Church, very much. We go there together Sunday and Wed. nights and he also sings Sunday mornings in the Methodist choir, and is an officer in the Epworth League. His Christianity certainly is real, for he is as kind to everyone as one could be. His Spanish, Mexican and Greek workmen at the mill evidently adore him. I think he is the only absolutely democratic person I've ever known anywhere.

Did I tell you his full name? It is John John Planwydd Roberts. I judge from little things he has said that his family are the leaders in their community, which is a little Welsh village with an interesting countryside where titled individuals have homes.

Sunday:

Read your second letter to-day. Wish I could accommodate you, Honey, but I haven't enough money now. Have that $300 mortgage, and then only $125 or so on 6 month deposit here, and am saving the rest for summer expenses, to begin getting trousseau, etc. I'm awfully sorry. If I were to teach next year perhaps I could manage it, but fear not as it is, unless you sold my present mortgage for me. Hope your plans will work out well.

I'm sorry to have to hurry so now. Yesterday helped Mrs. Gold entertain the M.E. ladies for Minna and this afternoon we were out from about 1:30 to 6 with the Golds in their machine, Jack, Minna, and I, with a picnic meal.

Indeed I do feel we have grown much closer together, dear, and hope this new event will make us much closer. I hope you can go to Commencement. You might write Miss Perry and ask her if you could have Dorothy in hall. Helen and I wanted to be together there and we could all have one room probably

More Later. Excuse haste.

Much Love, Elsie

April 15, Sat. Cleaned house and did some washing. Assisted at the pleasant afternoon party. Jack came late in the evening.

April 16, Sun. Palm Sunday service. Then Jack , Minna and I went with the Golds toward Hell's canyon in their machine. Climbed a hill afoot. Picnic meal. Went to Methodist Church in the evening, and then Jack stayed a little.

April 17, Mon. Wrote Easter cards. Our recipe files for which Jack gave Minna the money, came. Our "drop-in" group came. We served raspberry syrup and Nabiscos. I mended. They teased me about Jack. Looked at M's hope chest, and I almost told my secret.

Letter from Elsie's father
Elsinore, Calif.
April 17, 1916

Dear Elsie,

    I am glad to know that you feel happy and hope that you will always have reason to feel that way on account of Jack. I know that you realize that getting married is serious business, and that you have a high standard, and would not marry any man unless you had every reason to believe that he was everything that he should be in regard to morals, past life, etc.

    I know that you have good judgment, but do you really know anything about the young man except what you have seen of him and what he has told you? I understand from your letters that your friends think well of him. I am glad that he expects to get work, and live in California. It seems strange that two of our daughters should fall in love with, and want to marry British subjects.

    I do not object to them on that account, but as a rule, they do not have as high a regard for women as Americans do. If you know that you love Jack and that he loves you, that is the main thing (provided of course that he is all right, and has the ability and willingness to provide for you). We are pleased to think that you will not have to look forward to teaching school always, it is pretty hard work for you, although I know you enjoy it in a way

We would not want you to teach another year because you think you ought to help us or anything of that kind. If you have made up your mind to get married and Jack's income is sufficient, and the signs are right go ahead. I hope your eyes are feeling better, rest them all you can and don't go out too much at night and tire them with bright lights. And get all the sleep you can, or need. I think it will be a good plan for you to stay in Long Beach, the way you spoke of during part of the hot weather, at least, provided you can afford it. Of course your mother could stay with you part of the time, and then you could come here when it got cooler and the change would be good for you. I am sorry we are not living in a better house. It seems to agree with us here and I do not mind the heat and I expect we will be here for some time. I suppose you won't get here before the last of June. Take good care of yourself and don't tire yourself too much traveling, etc., and keep calm. We have been trying to trade this place for something smaller and nearer Los Angeles, but have nothing in view just now.

With much Love and good wishes, PAPA

April 18, Tues. School dismissed early at noon because prominent suffragettes spoke here en route to the Canyon. I told one of them about my Susan B. Anthony letter and she begged me to mount the platform! [Elsie's aunt had given her a letter she had received from Susan B. Anthony.] When I refused, another talked about me by name in her speech! Mr. Boone called. In the evening, Jack and I drew rough house-plans, and I read him parts of letters.

April 19, Wed. Helped Minna buy a hat. Jack and I sorted out Kodak films, etc., and talked, and loved! I am unspeakably glad and thankful.

April 21, Fri. Good Friday Enjoying Emerson's <u>Compensation</u> in English III. Jack and I went to the service at St. John's Mission.

April 22, Sat. Housework. Pressed my pretty blue linen coat-dress my dear mother made, bought shoes, etc. Callers. Jack came late, and Earl Fortney came from choir practice with Minna. We copied recipes. E. F. disgusted me.

April 23, Sun. Easter Day. A wonderful day. Jack gave me roses. I gave him my picture in a silver frame. His rug for me has not come yet. Church in the morning with him, and also at night at M. E. Between services we went up our canyon by the stream. He comforted my tears for Ruth. I love him more and more.

April 25, Tues. Mabyn and I went to Mexican town to see about our lace. Jack helped me restring my coral beads in the evening. He left early. I'm weary.

April 26, Wed. Supper at the Hoffpauirs'. The old mother is dear. Jack and I teased aplenty. Revival service afterward which I did not care for. Jack and I talked late and seriously.

April 27, Thurs. In evening we "Drop-Ins" met at M. C.'s & I was more than teased because Jack came early for me. I talked with him about Karl, shall I see Karl? Jack stopped smoking this evening.

April 28, Fri. Jack came unexpectedly because flowers were sent me. Henry Johnson came home from church with M., so J. stayed late!

April 29, Sat. After being disturbed because I missed the usual word from home I received beautiful letters from mother and Aunt M. Read A. K. Green's Woman in the Alcove in "library" while waiting for mail. Jack called.

April 30, Sun. A wonderful day! Early League breakfast leaving home about six. Then J. and I climbed Bill Williams, and had lunch on the "saddle." Found 30 kinds of wild flowers. Then went the last miles through snow. Glorious! Slid part of way back. I felt I belonged in a tale of the north and the wilds. Rested since we got home at 4:10. Then J. came for late supper. We must have gone 12 or 14 miles.[41]

May 1, Mon. As my glasses were broken yesterday it's hard to go on with school.

---

41 The Epworth League often met early on Sunday mornings for a breakfast hike before morning church.

Some seventy years later Elsie recalled how the teachers really had to toe the mark in the circumspect town of Williams. When a few days later at the Women's Club it was commented that even the Forest Service hadn't gone up Bill Williams Mountain due to the snow, she had to remain quiet. She couldn't tell anyone that the two of them had gone up together alone.

May 2, Tues. Jack came late and left early, but the time we had was good.

May 3, Wed. Our "Drop-Ins" met at the Watson's. The girls were kinder in their teasing, but Roy W. was worse!

May 4, Thurs. Jack went with me to collect books of mine left at the library. He told me more interesting things about his family and name.

May 6, Sat. Got two square meals for my guests. Enjoyed the guests ever so much. Ironed my middy and almost completely packed my trunk. We're going to leave Arcadia to let Nita and F. come. My Easter gift from Jack, beautiful Indian rug came. He went with me to meet Minna.

May 7, Sun. Jack and I climbed the hill back of "S. O. Miller of Buffalo." Went to League, and talked there. We stayed for church.

May 8, Mon. Packed further. Had a delightful time over my notebook planning and listing for hope chest.

May 9, Tues. The last night at Arcadia! Cleaned room, etc., packed. At school the enthusiasm over Merchant of Venice pleased me. Jack here for our last evening in this little house.

May 10, Wed. At the Gold's. Received and answered letter from E. Barron that made me feel queer! Went to Arcadia after school for final leaving. Nita and Ferd moved in and now I am feeling restful and at home in this pleasant room with Minna's room next to it.

May 11, Thurs. Even the children have heard my happy "secret!" I am disgusted that Lu is evidently to take my work next year, tho she has had no college education.[42] What a town! The Golds, Minna and I had a delightful picnic supper by the head of the dam. We gathered flowers there.

May 12, Fri. Beset with questions by Lois, Minnie, and Jane as to my engagement! I didn't tell. Went with Jack to picture-show Matrimony and a comic play. Said goodnight over the gate!

---

42 In *Ranch Schoolteacher* Eulalia Bourne wrote, "I had no college degree, no high school diploma, no elementary certificate. At that time almost anybody who could read could become a teacher. There was a minimum age limit of eighteen."

May 13, Sat. Heard we are not going to the Canyon on the Bass trip. Jack, Minna and I went to the school and played the Victrola. Jack and I walked by the dam.

May 14, Sun. Church and a rest. Then J. and I followed our stream farther than ever. Found white violets. Jack sang "Mother Mackree" as a solo for Mother's Day at M. E. Church. I was proud of him. Took some of our wild flowers to Mrs. Hoffpauir, and then we walked all the way through the canyon in moonlight.

Mother's Day
May 14, 1916

Dearest Mother,

It is too late for me to write you the long letter I planned, but I must say a little to you before I go to bed. I can never tell you how much I love you. I wish I could! When I think about marrying I appreciate you more, and Father too. I wish I could ever repay even a part of all you have done for me. The highest blessings you have given me I feel are those of spiritual emphasis and idealism. I don't see how parents could give anything better than that, and those I have certainly had from my father and mother. This morning I went to my church, and tonight to the Special Mother's Day one at the Methodist church. Tho Jack isn't used to singing solos he sang well. I rested this afternoon for a while, but we walked all the later part of the afternoon. The wild flowers are glorious! Some are kinds new to me. We walked again in the moonlight after church.

Jack expects to write to you and Father tomorrow. I hope you'll both answer soon, as I know he'll be rather anxious to hear from you! People here are finding out so much, taking so much for granted, etc. that we thought it would be more sensible to acknowledge it. Some of my schoolgirls keep telling me they hear we are engaged, and begging me to tell them if it's true or not! Poor Jack doesn't know how to write his letter. He says he's never written one that was neither business-like, stiff, nor humorous. His have always been one of the three and humorous if they were friendly. He says since this can't have any of those qualities he doesn't know how to write it. He's more full of fun than any other person I've ever known, tho at heart he is deeply serious. He is so generous and kind-hearted that I feel very selfish beside him. I love him more all the time.

Last night Nita and Ferd, Jack, M. and I went to the schoolhouse and played the Victrola. J. and I went to the picture show Friday. Now the Golds have offered their den for us for evenings. We took some of our wild flowers to old Mrs. Hoffpauir this evening.

Thank you both again for what you offer as to the lot. We both think you are too generous. We can talk about that when I see you.

I hope you won't have a hard time getting used to the new teeth, Honey.

We've found we aren't going to the Canyon, so after a few days at Cornville I'll probably come home for a few more before Commencement, say from the 12th to the 16th or 17th. Then after Commencement Jack might go back to Elsinore with me for two days or so, of course I'd stay longer. Would that suit you? I can hardly wait to have you all meet him. I think you'll like him and admire his character so much that you won't mind any little primitive ways he may still have left after his years in the wilds. He was 270 miles from a railroad for 3 years! He knows every kind of life, tho, more or less, and has seen something of the most entirely fashionable society, which disgusted him, as well as the rough wilds.

I hope your foot is quite well. I'm delighted that Alice, Ernest, and Dorothy are to visit you soon. I just wish they could still be there the 12th! It is lovely of you to share the carnations. Did Father order the white ones for today himself? Thank you for the enclosures. I hope you aren't any of you working too hard.

Please tell Aunt Mamie I appreciated her note very much. Jack thinks because she is so merry that they'll be good comrades. Nita gave M. and me each a pretty towel for our chests.

> With very much love to you and
> Father and Aunt Mamie, Elsie

May 15, Mon. At Mabyn Chapman's. At school Lois discovered that I have measles (German ones), so I saw Dr. Jeffries and came here, not daring to go home for Myra's sake. Wrote Jack about it, odd to write to him! Slept in the afternoon. Philip and I have changed beds for a while. Lois brought book and flowers.

May 16, Tues. Minna again brought my dinner from Mrs. Parker and with it a letter from Jack. He enclosed one to Father and Mother, which I sent on to them. Wrote him again, and other letters. I'm speckled all over! Lois came, and Marie, with candy. Lulu called, briefly. Everyone is very good to me. I don't feel very ill.

May 17, Wed. Again a letter from Jack at noon, and I wrote him. Called on Hollis Patterson who also has measles. Walked a little. Jack came, tho he "kept his distance!" We walked a little, but he went very early.

Letter from Jack

My Dear little Sweetheart,

   I did not know what to think today when the girls sent word to me that you were sick, that you really had the measles. I had just been pondering what to write to Pa. Here is what I wrote so if you approve of it you can send it or if you want to change anything send it back and I'll doctor it up.

   I told Ferguson today I was going away. I am very anxious to hear from your parents to hear what they will have to say.

   Hope you will feel fine tomorrow.

                    With Love from Yours Ever, Jack

May 18, Thurs. Read in <u>Memoirs of Sherlock Holmes</u> and <u>Pollyanna Grown Up</u>. Couldn't go to Minna's shower, but had a lovely evening with my beau.

May 19, Fri. The Gold's again. Wrote many letters, came back to the Gold's. I've missed Minna, and am glad to be with her again.

May 20, Sat. Minna went to the lumber camps, but rain and my measles cold kept me at home, where I disinfected. At night Jack and I talked with Mrs. Gold and Minna here, walked, went to choir practice, and got ice cream.

May 21, Sun. Tramped to Three Hills, Jack and I, a glorious trip. He sang well in a quartet at church. Hess' ice cream again. My mouth still sore from measles. His letter came from my father and mother and we feel better. Walked again. Some disturbing thoughts come across the new happiness.

May 22, Mon. Back at school again. Minna and I met Jack by chance and he treated us to ice cream at Hess' and Lebsch's both! We called on the Sines. They begged me to let them "announce" Sat!

May 23, Tues. I remember my dear "other members" [the Triumvirate] and am grateful for God's gifts. Jack took a party of us three to the Box Factory and then helped me copy recipes. We talked late in the Gold's kitchen.

May 24, Wed. Lois gave me a Hope Chest gift that is embarrassing! On our way to "Drop In" at Sugar's Jack took the group of us into Mr. Hess' for sundaes! I am teased further.

May 25, Thurs. Went with Jack and a little girl, Norah Buss, to League party. We walked afterward.

May 26, Fri. Full day at school and worked on exam questions afterward. Jack took a group of us through the mill. Then we walked by the dam. Lights wonderful.

May 27, Sat. On Mother's birthday my engagement was announced at a luncheon given by Mrs. Sine. Before that we went to a breakfast shower for Mary given by Mrs. Jeffries. Then I heard that a little brother or sister is expected for Dorothy! I feel much.

The *Williams News*
ANNOUNCEMENT LUNCHEON

Saturday Mrs. A. Sine and Miss Sine entertained at luncheon in honor of the Misses Mary Collins, Minna Wissing and Elsie Hayes, all brides-elect. Shasta daisies decorated the table and helped carry out the color scheme of white and gold. Hearts in the same color were strung from the chandeliers and bore the monograms of the betrothed couples.

In the center of the table a miniature ship, "Matrimony," sailed on a peaceful sea and carried a cargo of daisies, hearts and secrets. Smaller ships designated places, were moored by golden ropes to tiny posts hidden in the green along the edge of the sea.

Cleverly concealed under a covering of daisies and green foliage was the first course, a fruit cocktail, while throughout the luncheon the courses were served in original style. The ice cream was attractive in tiny baskets of cake, the handles of which were decorated with gilded wishbones and white ribbons.

Between courses the time flew merrily disclosing the secrets of the table and the ship. The pilings were found to contain prophecies and character sketches of all present. But the greatest surprise was the message borne by the ship "Matrimony" which was disclosed by the pulling of its overflowing cargo of hearts to which were attached double hearts announcing the engagement of Miss Elsie Reed Hayes to Mr. J. P. Roberts. This called forth great applause as it was so unexpected and later brought showers of rice. A bridal cake was then set before the guests of honor and cut by Miss Hayes, much amusement being afforded by the finding of the significant tokens hidden therein.

Saturday, May 27, 1916

Dearest Family,

My engagement has been formally announced. Mrs. Sine (and Grace and Mrs. Sweetwood) were giving a luncheon today, and asked me to let them announce it then. They knew, because Grace used to go with Jack and he knows all of them, as that I told them. This morning there was a breakfast given for Mary, a shower, at 9:45. Then at 1 P.M. we all went to the luncheon, all but one the same crowd, about 14 girls. Both were elegant meals, with elaborate place-cards, etc. I'll tell you more about them when I see you.

At the luncheon my name and J's were on little hearts in a beautiful paper ship used with flowers as a centerpiece. Ribbons attached to other hearts were pulled all at once between courses. Then the "brides elect," especially myself, were showered with rice. I thought you wouldn't mind, as the consent was given to our engagement! The girls shouted!

Your letter came after I began this. I am surprised about Alice, but I think so she doesn't have too many it is fine to have two near together, better for the babies by far. I'll send her a note. Unless she wants to announce again for me in Calif. (and I think she better not try now!) you may tell it now to anyone you like.

Wednesday the League (which I'm to lead tomorrow) is to give a farewell party to Minna, Martha Moore, Jack, and me, the four of us. There's to be a school program, etc.

Thursday eve: M. expects to leave Fri. noon, Jesse to meet her in Chicago. She doesn't know when she'll be married, perhaps very soon.

I got Helen to bring me a new waist in L.A., voile, pretty, $1.98. I may send my party dress by mail to avoid crushing. It needs changing, the adding of a pink slip I can make easily before commencement from my old pink dress or my pink petticoat. If it comes please shake it out and hang up, covered by a sheet. Please ask the postmaster to put with your mail any coming to me, and open and read and save any magazines. Don't send letters to me here to reach here after June 2 unless I tell you differently later. Haven't made final arrangements with Mrs. Hurst, but expect still to be there about a week.

Jack is looking after my books, and a big box of them and bedding will arrive sometime.

Yes, I think that last picture is good of Jack. My eyes seem better. Dorothy must be adorable!

Doesn't it seem odd that it happens to be on your birthday that my engagement was announced? I'm glad to have it so. I hope you have had a lovely day.

Tuesday

And this still un-mailed! We're going to Mrs. Plummer's to luncheon to-day, and we're going to Mrs. Boone's for dinner, but she has measles. Jack and I were deluged with congratulations and good wishes at both churches Sunday. I led League, Jack took M. and me to the Fray Marcos for dinner, and he and I tramped in the afternoon.

I still have not heard finally from Mrs. Hurst. I do hope Alice and Dorothy will still be at Elsinore when I get there. It will probably be about a week from Monday, for I suppose I'll go to Mrs. Hurst this coming Saturday. I'll tell you later about mail.

I hope you are all well. The chickens must be fine.

There's to be a school program Thursday night to which Jack and I expect to come.

With very much love to you all, Elsie.
Please send this to Hylinda, I'm sorry
Ernest could not stay longer at the ranch.
Don't let D. get hold of my letters.
There must be measles germs at school!

May 28, Sun. Deluged with good wishes and congratulations at my church in the morning, Jack's at night, and between. He took Minna and me to dinner at the Fray Marcos. We said goodbye to our stream and climbed the cliffs above it. We went to Harvey House and walked.

May 29, Mon. Jack and I walked on the canyon road, and climbed the cliffs. Mariposa tulips and fireflies. I love him!

May 30, Tues. Eighth grade state examinations. Cheating saddened us. Were to go to a dinner party at Mrs. Boone's but she had measles.

May 31, Wed. Receiving more Hope Chest gifts, including booties from the schoolgirls! Packed. Party given as farewell for M. Moore, Minna, Jack, and me. Too many good things said about us!

June 2, Fri. Had to make another unexpected speech, this time to the Assembly. Hard to say goodbye to children. Hard to say it to Minna. Called on Mrs. Udin, Mr. Boone, Mrs. Robinson, Mrs. Watson, Mrs. Ericson, Mary and Georgia, Nita. Good walk with Jack.

June 3, Sat. The Hursts'. Oak Creek. Jack and others saw me off. With Philip to Ash Fork. With Mr Hoffpauir to Cedar Glade. Met by Mr. and Mrs. Hurst at Clarkdale. After supper we drove to their ranch, getting here at 11:30. I am serene.

June 4, Sun. Revel in the tots. Talked and rested. Children and their elders talked as they passed horseback and some came in, though Harriett has German measles.

June 5, Mon. Played on the lawn with the children, washed dishes, talked and rested. I am glad I came. I think constantly of my Jack.

June 6, Tues. E. Barron came and was invited for overnight. He told me I ought to spend my honeymoon in the cottage on the upper ranch! [Said sarcastically because the cottage belonged to Karl.] Life is strange. I enjoyed him, but could hardly wait for the mail that brought a letter from Jack. It was good.

June 7, Wed. Mr. Barron and I talked most of the day on the porch, but washed dishes besides. Went swimming in the creek with the children and had a nap after he left. I feel like someone else. Mrs. Hurst is wonderful.

June 8, Thurs. Wrote letters, talked and rested, gathered peaches, hung clothes on the line. Rufus Hill called on me!

June 9, Fri. Repacked my suitcases. Cut paper-doll dresses for Harriet and Edna, and talked with Ruth seriously while we worked. Rode horseback to Cornville PO with Mrs. Page. Wrote Alice M. Parker. I feel much.

June 10, Sat. Mrs. Hurst drove me to the post office, and we talked of Karl. I can't express how much I honor her. Helped stage driver deliver and get mail bags. Nine or ten miles auto to Clarkdale, then 3 train lines to Williams. Jack met me, we walked to the lumber yard. Saw Nita's little son, and rejoice for her, about three days old.

June 11, Sun. So good to be with Jack again! Gathered Mariposas and walked. Farewells. Train (no. 7) left at midnight-day coach! Mexican seat-mate awhile!

June 12, Mon. ELSINORE Slept better than I had dared hoped without a bed! Wrote to Jack. Breakfast at Barstow. Lunch at Riverside with Marjorie. At 6:30 met by Father and Mother, then came out to the ranch, seeing Aunt Mamie. Good to be home!

June 13, Tues. Oh so good to be here! Talk and talk of Jack. Lazy day Unpacked, etc. and showed things.

June 15, Thurs. Mother painted my quaint old hope chest, and she and Aunt Mamie embroidered etc. for me. My family is good to me! I keep thinking of Jack as here.

June 16, Fri. Claremont, got ready for Claremont Pomona Commencement and left at noon. Wire from Jack that his train was late. Jack came late at night. Joy to have him.

June 19, Mon. Jack and I sat in the gallery for Commencement. The "Dog and the Slush" for dinner. Took Jack to meet May Lovely things about him have been said to me. Father met us at Elsinore, we were embarrassed! Talked late.

June 21, Wed. Wonderfully happy Went after alfalfa hay by auto, Father, Jack and I raked! Climbed the favorite hill at sunset. It is wonderful to have him here.

June 22, Thurs. Went in machine to Cold Water canyon, 12 miles, a glorious place. After dinner Jack and I tramped, following the stream. Tangles of grapevine. Stopped for Matilijas and Larkspurs on way home. Poor Friskie is sick. Jack means more to me all the while.

June 24, Sat. Jack rowed me on the lake and over it. We made "hay" together again. We stay up late every night.

June 25, Sun. We all went to church. Jack and I made a "house" in the eucalyptus grove, rested in it. I surely can't say what I feel!

June 30, Fri. Long Beach Jack and I left on early train. He re-established himself with the Elks in L.A. while I shopped. Saw Pavlovian picture show.

July 6, Thurs. Worked a little. Met Jack about 3:30 and walked on beach and ate supper with him. He has accepted a position at Wilmington. Heard good news through Mrs. Hurst.

July 10, Mon. Came here to Staileys'. There's an ache in my throat, but I am grateful for Ruth and for Jack. First evening without him, after twenty three together unbroken.

Aug. 18, Fri. Fanny and I went downtown, had lunch there, and read in the library We went to Pomona college reunion at the Yeoman's home, about

26 girls and 3 men! Some of the freshmen to-be promise well. Heard that Karl called to see me this summer, but found me gone.

Aug. 23, Wed. Aunt Mamie took the eight of us to dinner at Strand Cafe. Then went to a movie. Jack came late for a call. I do love Him!

Sept. 5, Tues. Took the day lazily to rest, but wrote down lists, wedding ideas that came to me, etc. The Diary reminds me of two years ago. How strange is life, hard and glad!

Sept. 13, Wed. Mother and I went up to the city and had lunch at the Staileys'. Shopped a little, bought beautiful pink crepe de chine for my negligee.

LONG BEACH
October 1, 1916

Dear Family,

I did some more shopping last week, including a cream serge skirt to wear now. I got a white silk petticoat for my trousseau for $1.95. I also got a bungalow apron housedress etc. It is lots of fun. Jack was here last evening. We went to the house on Hill St. we've engaged and asked questions. There is no coop, but wire that the landlady said could be used for one. I think it would be fine to bring some chickens. She furnishes bedding and towels, dishes and silver, etc. We can have the house Fri. I hope you'll like it. It's in need of paint but has pretty lawn. It is pleasantly furnished and has a singer sewing machine we may use. It is $10.00 a month and water making $11.30. Her gas and light last month were only .90 cents there are stores near and Methodist and Baptist churches.

With hope of seeing some of you soon.

I am Very lovingly your Elsie

ELSINORE

Oct. 24, Tues. Two rabbits in traps last night. Fine sleeping out-of-doors. Helped with the wash, went to the village with Joe (the horse). Read <u>Dreams</u>. Heard that Mr. Youngblood is married. Bob Bell and LuLu M. engaged.

Oct. 27, Fri. It seems a little lonely, just Aunt Mamie and I on the ranch. Cooked a little, sewed, etc. We harnessed Joe and I drove to town. Another dear letter from my Jack. One from Mrs. Hurst.

Letter from Jack
Oct. 27
Crocker St. Los Angeles

Dear Sweetheart,

Well I am still on the job. Been here over a week now and I don't think I'll change. I could get about $80.00 a month. I was glad to learn you were so successful with your traps. I hope you will keep on, you will make a hunter yet. Everyone thinks business will pick up after elections so a fellow will have a better chance to make money. Say do you realize it is a year ago since I first met or saw you? Here we are not married yet but that will come soon. Send me a piece of paper the size of your finger as I will have to get your ring made for you. I never thought I would be in California of all places; and especially as happy as I am. I don't know how you feel but I believe if my suspenders would break I would go straight up.

No more news, everybody down here is talking elections and I can't vote so I am just mad.

Well today the foreman asked me if he quit to go to another job if I would go with him. He said he was pretty sure he would be able to start me at $18.00 per week.

That is certainly a nice letter you sent my folks. They will be dippy over you yet. But why shouldn't they? I know I am.

From yours ever, Jack

October 31, Tues. Thought lovingly of Minna today. How I wish her plans were still like mine! Went with father in machine around end of the lake for grain and helped get hay on the way back. Fine letter from Jack, little thought what ring meant that I drew in cake a year ago today! In letter today Jack asked ring size.

November 13, Mon. Decided not to go back to Elsinore today, as Alice needs me. Played maid, kitchen girl and nurse girl. "Phoned to Jack." Two Years ago I last saw Karl, I remember.

November 20, Mon. From Long Beach went back to Elsinore. Went to Los Angeles and shopped a little, then took bus for Elsinore. During puncture delay in dark found my fellow passenger is a friend of the Hursts and Karl. How strange it all is!

November 21, Tues. I notice this day on other years. Within one year that began three years ago were all my seeings of Karl. How much more Jack has changed the world for me in less than a year!

December 1, Fri. Finished new cover for comfort, helped gather vegetables, and bring in wood. I think especially of Ruthie again. Betrothal announcement from Mr. Latham and Mildred Murphy. Did I do all my duty?

December 2, Sat. Made pies, swept and dusted. Mother and I drove Joe to town. Letter from Mrs. Hurst and her lovely hope chest gift to me, a silk "nightie" with crochet. Particularly good letter from Jack. She sent one from Karl.

Letter from Jack
Los Angeles

Dear Sweetheart,

Last night I went out in the rain and did my Christmas shopping as far as my money went. I am sending to the Old Country with yours and mine Christmas greetings.

I feel fine these days and happy to be thinking of the future. I hope it won't be long until we are able to settle down in a place of our own. After

Christmas I am going to be sending you about $10.00 a week and when you get enough you can say so. I'll be ready anytime you are.

Remember me kindly to your Papa and give my love to your mother and Aunt Mamie.

With Sincerest Love from
your own Sweetheart, Jack

December 11, Mon. Jack's Birthday. I love him dearly. Some things I cannot put in my diary!

December 13, Wed. Want Jack, and am eager to be married, yet hate to think of leaving my family. Letter from Jack made date of wedding seem more certain. So hard to arrange by mail!

December 15, Fri. Packed more. Letter from Jack deciding me positively on Christmas Day. Went with family to church supper. "Asked the minister."

December 20, Wed. Preparations for my wedding and for Christmas. It doesn't seem real.

December 22, Fri. Busy again! I hate to think of leaving home, but it will be good to be with Jack! Hylinda came, good to have her.

December 23, Sat. Jack came while I was helping decorate. We went to the village and got the license. Heard this was the day Minna and Jesse were married.

December 24 Sun. Rain and restfulness. Directed the last announcements. Hylinda played and we all sang hymns, lovely family day.

December 25, 1916 Mon. Our Wedding Day! The living room was lovely with green and white. Mr. Hunt preformed the ceremony, only the family there. Then Christmas wedding dinner and the tree. Amsbury Hotel, Elsinore for all night. The threads of my life!

Epilogue

Jack and Elsie

Elsie Reed Hayes lived in southern California after her marriage to Jack Roberts. She never returned to Oak Creek or to Arizona. In 1918 Jack and Elsie and their baby daughter Catherine (my mother) moved to Palomar Mountain, California. They operated the family apple ranch and later opened a resort on the ranch called Planwydd. In 1924 they moved down the mountain to San Diego in order for Catherine to attend school, although they maintained a lifelong connection to Palomar.

Elsie wrote short stories for children's publications and later worked as a librarian. Years later, after Jack's death in 1947 at the age of fifty-seven, Elsie twice visited his family in Wales. She wrote in her trip diary, "As a girl I had been bewitched by tales of Arthur. Over and over I had read Tennyson's 'Idylls of the King.' In college Alice Parker had a tremendous interest in the Celts. All this may have been one reason why I fell in love with Jack, the ardent Welsh lover. Jack and his ancestors lived at the foot of Mt. Snowdon."

Jack, who left his home and family when he was only sixteen years old, never returned to visit his family in Wales. He was Catrin and Griffith Roberts' only son. As a mother of three sons I have wondered how I would have felt if one of my sons had left home at age sixteen, never to return. There may have been good reasons for this. In 1916, when Jack was twenty-six and married Elsie, he was still establishing himself. World War I had broken out, and travel to Wales would have been nearly impossible. Jack's father wrote to him that jobs were scarce in their little village, but that he hoped someday Jack could bring his bride Elsie to visit.

Later, Jack's parents longed to meet Catherine, their only granddaughter, but for a number of years the apple ranch and resort took all of Jack and Elsie's time. By the 1930s the depression meant that there was no money for travel. Then World War II came along, again rendering travel to Wales difficult, if not impossible. When Elsie finally went to Wales she was in her mid-seventies, and only Jack's cousins remained alive to meet her. She loved Wales and meeting those who still remembered her husband.

er Dan, my sister Nancy, and I were privileged to be Elsie's
. Our beloved grandmother died just six months short of her
h birthday in July 1987. She always considered her "Arizona
ler favorite. Her letters, tied with a faded, tattered blue ribbon,
and her well-worn journal contained her priceless memories. She always
encouraged me to write, and so I have tried to tell her story.

Karl Hurst

Elsie's tears at my question proved she never forgot Karl. When my
manuscript for this book was nearly completed a librarian sent me a treasure
found in the University of Arizona's archives. It was a page from the 1917
annual showing Karl Hurst's name on the honor roll and a picture of him in
the Delta Phi fraternity. So, after his time spent in the mental institution, he
returned to the university and finished another year of college. While in the
university, on March 25, 1916, he enlisted in the National Guard, Co. 1, 1st
Arizona infantry. On August 5, 1917, four months after the United States
entered World War I his unit was activated into federal service and was sent
to France in the summer of 1918.

Memorial Fountain University of Arizona, Tucson

Karl's mother mailed to Elsie a small memorial card which reads, "On the field of honor in beloved France, Karl T. Hurst gave his life gloriously for liberty and democracy." On January 31, 1920, US General John J. Pershing dedicated the Berger Memorial Fountain just west of Old Main on the University of Arizona, Tucson, campus. The large memorial fountain is dedicated to the thirteen Sons of the University of Arizona who answered their country's call for service and gave their lives in the World War of 1917–18. This fountain is erected with enduring affection in honor of:

Alexander Tindolph Berger
Morgan Bland McDermott
James Preston Jones
Hugh Daye Campbell
Leslie Abram Waterbury
Louis Edward Kengla
Leonard Low

Karl Thomas Hurst
William Orville Bloys
Cornelis Molenbeek
Ritchie William Jones
Corlande Brown Curry
Homer Donald Whipp

It was a solemn moment when I visited the memorial fountain and saw Karl's name listed among the thirteen students who died in WW1. This sensitive, brave cowboy-turned-scholar-turned-soldier is still remembered.

Colleagues

Marguerite Melick and Minna Wising, Elsie's two roommates, were not mentioned again in Elsie's writings and no further information could be obtained regarding them.

The Girdners

When I met Eva Girdner Stone in December 1988, she still lived on Shadyvale Ranch. She was eighty-seven years "young." I traveled to the same Girdner farm where Elsie had lived seventy-five years before.

Eva shared many delightful remembrances of that time. "My mother always used white linen tablecloths so as to teach us children to be careful in our eating habits. She charged us ten cents if we spilled a drop of blackberry juice as it wouldn't wash out. School supplies were almost nonexistent. We had a reader, an arithmetic, a speller, a geography and history book, and we almost knew them by heart at the close of the year. We all had slates for school. For groceries or 'boughten' things we had to go to Jerome, which took all day in a lumber wagon. We only went a few times a year."

Eva died in 1998.

Stanley Girdner was ninety years old and was also living on Shadyvale Ranch when I visited there in 1988. He explained that the roads to Jerome were so rough that his father always traveled with road repair tools—picks, chains, and sometimes dynamite. Stanley also recalled his brother Glen placing a red ribbon in his red hair at school one day. Miss Melick told him to remove it or go home. When she turned her back, Glen jumped out of the schoolhouse window, ran around the school and then climbed back in. He also described how when the children were "scrapping," all the other children would form a ring around the fighting boys. Miss Melick once tried to get inside the ring by pounding on the children's hands.

Stanley was still winning and handsome when I met him some seventy-five years after Elsie had known him. He lived to be one hundred years old.

Other Cornville students

Nellie May Smith (Hart) was still living in Cottonwood in 1988. She was eighty-eight years old. Her memories of Elsie were sweet. Nellie recalled how the entire class used a single granite cup to dip water from the bucket in the school. "No one was ever sick. We had a lot of fun." Although Nellie's little sister Della (for whom Elsie had written a poem) was sound asleep when it was time for her to say her piece for the Christmas program in 1913, a year later when Elsie returned to Cornville for Christmas vacation, she arrived the night of the Christmas program just in time to hear Della recite the poem she had written.

Ed Lee, another Cornville student, was living in Prescott in 1988 when I had a memorable visit with him. He was then eighty-two years old. He died in 1998.

Wiley Stewart was living in Jamul, California, in 1988. He also shared memories with me in letters. He recounted that most of the children walked to school, though some rode horses or burros. He wrote to me, "Miss Hayes was one of my favorite teachers."

Others

Elsie's niece Dorothy Burley McCune is 96 years old and living in California.

Elsie's sister Hylinda married Absolom Urshan from Persia.

Eugene Barron, the Red Rock school teacher, died in the flu epidemic of 1918.

Frank Gold, the lawyer who was sent to Arizona in 1913 to die of tuberculosis ended up living in Flagstaff for many years after he left Williams. His daughter Myra died at age fourteen.

W.W. Bass, Grand Canyon guide. Born in Indiana in 1849, Mr. Bass came West in 1880. He continued his Grand Canyon business until 1923, dying in 1933.

The 1910 census for Yavapai County was 17,000 people or two people per square mile. Jerome in 1913 had a population of 3,000. In 1911 there were 535 primary schools in Arizona. There were 876 teachers for 38,611 children ages 6 through 21.

The following teachers were listed on the Williams school letterhead stationery for 1914: Elsie Hayes (6&7th grades), Minna Wissing (4&5th grades), LuLu Keating (3rd grade), Juanita Reese (2nd grade), Lava Sughrue (1st grade American), Mary Collins (1st grade Mexican), Bertha Peet (music & drawing) and Mary Watson (manual training). Georgia Alcorn was the principal and J. S. Campbell, E. M. Twitty, and Mrs. Andrew Miller were the trustees.

The historical markers database lists the following stores in Williams in 1914: a dime store, Duffy Brothers grocery store, Adams Grocery, Grand Canyon drugstore (which included a soda fountain in the front and a doctor's office in the rear), Rittenhouse haberdashery (a men's clothing store), and Babbitt Polson general store. The Sultana was an entertainment center that included a saloon, billiard hall, buffet, and theater. The Pollock building included the newspaper and telegraph office. The opera house was built in 1912, and the library was constructed in 1915.

The *Williams News* reported in 1915, "Williams Opera house—Old Fashioned Dance—Price including supper .50 cents. Hardwood floor has been cleaned and sandpapered."

Perhaps Elsie's mentor, Alice Parker, had been thinking of Elsie when she wrote this poem that I discovered among Elsie's Arizona memoirs.

Sonnet to a Beautiful Woman
By Alice M. Parker

The rarest beauty in a woman's face
Grows from the blended touch of artists twain:
And one is sorrow whose firm strokes of pain
The lines of sympathy and courage trace.
Sharp angles carved by suffering round to curves
That witness peace and inward victory,
Won by strong hearts that struggle mightily.
With patient fortitude that never swerves.

That is love's light new-kindled in the eyes
From which the sweet, surrendered soul looks out;
The tender pencilings about the lips
Are drawn there by love's gracious fingertips;
A radiance like a halo shines about
The joy-lit face supreme Love glorifies.

The poem below was written in 1904 by Elsie to Caroline Harnett three years before Caroline died in a kitchen fire.

To Caroline

When, in the years to come,
We shall be old,
And our glad lives will be
Tales that are told,
May we remember

School-days of yore!
The lessons, the old games,
The mystical lore
Which mingles with fact
In a little girl's heart,
The loves, and the longings—
All these were a part
Of our happy school life,
Far happier made
Because 'twas together
We studied and played

Elsie wrote "Haunted" sometime after her marriage to Jack.

Haunted

There are those who fear shapes in the darkness,
Those who tremble at dream visitations—
Ah, but I—I am haunted by beauty,
When the past and absent are present,
And with magic of memory mountains
Far away, long unseen, rise about me.
In the blackness of night, tossing, sleepless,
(Then when all things are hidden, and seen, too;)
Or perchance it may be at mid-morning,
As from prosaic floors dust is garnered,
They are there: sudden, vivid, a vision.
Autumn leaves on a trail that winds, climbing;
High above, swaying evergreen branches;
Shining vistas of breath-taking grandeur;
Frail wild flowers by waterfalls nodding.
I hear birdcalls and wind in the forest,
Catch the tang and fragrance of mountains.
What a boon, to be haunted by beauty!

Acknowledgements

I am so thankful that the Lord allowed me the blessing of being Elsie's granddaughter. She was an amazing grandmother and a master storyteller.

What an adventure it has been to go back in time and discover for myself the history surrounding her years in Arizona. It was a privilege to actually meet four of Elsie's former students and interview them in 1988. It was thrilling to read letters from others who knew of the Cornville School in its early days. These elderly Arizonans shared their vivid memories of a life in that State which has long since disappeared. Eva Girdner Stone continued to write to me for quite a few years.

This project has seen four generations working together to tell this story. Elsie wrote and left behind her manuscript describing her adventures. My parents Katie and Chuck Beishline traveled with me to Arizona to discover the mystery hidden in Elsie's letters and diary. My son Dan Waite drew the pen and ink illustrations in 1989. Dan also scanned Elsie's photos and his wife Peichi did proofreading. My daughter Carin Roylance was an invaluable help with the wording of the final manuscript. My husband Curt and sons Christopher and Josh all encouraged me as I spent hours laboring on "the project."

Perhaps Elsie's love of adventure and teaching was passed on to me as well as to my children. I spent years living on the little island of Antigua, teaching our four children. Now, two of our children are involved in international education. All of our children inherited Elsie's love of adventure and literature. I occasionally wrote articles telling of my own experiences and Elsie was my cheerleader.

My sister Nancy Beishline, my brother Dan and sister-in-love Marcia Beishline helped with photos and documents, wording and encouragement.

To compile these precious memories and photographs seemed a daunting task. Yet I felt compelled to complete this Arizona story that Elsie had begun to write about in her last years. It has only been possible to accomplish because of all the many "guardian angels" the Lord has provided to help me. A few years ago I spoke to a women's group called Grandmothers in Touch. I challenged them to leave behind a written testimony of what the

Lord has done in their lives. This compelled me to set out once again on the "Elsie Project." Over the years several precious friends helped me type the manuscript. Thank you to Shirley Reese and Anna Lou Wren. I remain a two-finger typist. Janet Shay of Sable Creek Press encouraged me to "get back in the saddle again" and complete this book. She provided invaluable advice. Wonderful friends Bill and Helen Reid provided housing when we visited former students in 1988. Thanks to Judy Hong for advice on the business end of all this. Thanks to Diane King for creating a cover worthy of Elsie. Steve Skaggs assisted with editing and Greta Rohrer with proofing. Stephen Moody was a great help in managing my website. Jackie Neal at Palmetto Graphics assisted with printing my brochures. I give thanks to Mary Medlen for always encouraging me.

Kathleen Schmand of Northern Arizona University helped with research by providing newspaper articles from Williams. Jill McCleary and Crystal Carpenter also provided research help.

I look forward to compiling the story of Elsie's adventures as she and Jack operated an apple ranch and then Planwydd resort on Palomar Mountain in the early 1900s.

On my website www.barbaraannewaite.com I have included some tid-bits not included in *Elsie*. As I did research I discovered many interesting historical facts that make this fascinating time period come alive.

Thank you for reading *Elsie*. It has been my joy to share her with those who were not privileged to know and love her.

—Barbara Anne Waite

Bibliography

Arizona Bushmasters, Arizona Memory Project, Arizona State Library, http://azmemory.lib.az.us/cdm4/index.php?CISOROOT=/ammbush.

Arizona State University website, "Nature, Culture, and History at the Grand Canyon, http://grandcanyonhistory.clas.asu.edu/sites_rimview points_hopipoint.html.

Bass, William Wallace. *Rhymes and Jingles, The Grand Canyon Guide* (Los Angeles; J. F. Rowney Press, 1915).

Berkman, Pamela, ed. *History of Atchison, Topeka & Santa Fe* (Bromptom Books Corp., 1988).

Bourne, Eulalia. *Ranch School Teacher* (Tucson: University of Tucson Press, 1974).

Daniel, Clifton, ed. *Chronicle of the 20th Century* (New York: Chronicle Publications, 1987).

"Eastman Kodak Co." brochure, Rochester, NY, 1911.

Forest Lookouts website, http://westlookouts.weebly.com/arizona-a-d.html.

The Historical Markers Database, "Williams Markers," http://www.hmdb.org/results.asp?Town=Williams&State=Arizona (June 2011).

Jerome Community Service Organization, *Jerome Tourguide*.

Northern Arizona Fair Program, 28 October, 1913.

"Past Days," Sharlott Hall Museum, September 30, 2001.

Sonnichsen, C. L. *Tucson: The Life and Times of an American City* (Norman, OK: University of Oklahoma Press, 1982).

Thomas, Marshall. *The First Six Months of Prohibition in Arizona* (Tucson Print and Pub. Co., 1915).

Williams News, March 12, 1914.

Yavapai Monthly Magazine, January 15, 1915.

Tapia, John E. *Circuit Chautauqua* (North Carolina: McFarland,1996).

The Pike, http://en.wikipedia.org/wiki/The_Pike

CPSIA information can be obtained at www.ICGtesting.com
Printed in the USA
BVOW010659051111

275335BV00004B/1/P

9 780983 945208